LOVE IS HAPPINESS

Tomorrow's a New Day

Rosy Columbine

Motley Geekery

LOVE IS HAPPINESS

ISBN: **978-0-9929197-1-9**

Published by: Motley Geekery
43 Emmetts Park, Ashburton, Devon
TQ13 7DB

www.motleygeekery.co.uk

To John, David, Ben and Kate
with all my love.

Prologue

To John, David, Ben and Kate with all my love. How inadequate the words seem, when dealing with things that matter most, or with those whom you love. I can see you now in my mind's eye, as you were then, a friend of Kate's remarked upon it one day when you were all teenagers, we all thought we were quite different, but she said "No, you all have the same eyes, there is no mistaking it, exactly the same, anyone could tell you were family." We were genuinely amazed, and then I remembered once an Aunt by marriage, showing me the family portraits, "Look at the eyes," said she, "You can see straight away that you are all related!" Yours were the eyes that lit the feeling, showed the love, gleamed with mischief, conveyed so much joy and expressed so much when you were young and free-spirited. "They are so natural", everyone said of you, as if surprised, it pleased them though, and you all showed a genuine interest in whoever came to see us, young or old, you talked to them too and listened to their stories with pleasure, showed them the garden and told them about the things you did, and they enjoyed their visits and always told me how much good they felt it did them, to see you all, and go away much cheered.

Do you know how much I love you I wonder? Don't think about it, it's just that I get this ridiculous kind of yearning at times, when I want to give you love and happiness and joy, but that is probably a feeling that parents always have, and I believe it is with you anyway really, love is happiness so it makes me happy, it shouldn't be a burden to you, but a freedom, a freedom to be what you want, do what you want. I get such enormous happiness from the way you live your lives, you all work hard these days, but you retain the joy that you had then in simple things, being out in the countryside or the beach in all weathers, keeping your feet firmly on the ground, and joy in your hearts for the important things in this world, the things that money cannot buy. I never expected the wonderful family reunions we have had, when I gained strength and joy from you all just as I did when you were too young to know how much you gave.

It was a wonderful adventure while you were all growing up, and then... those childhood days were all over, it seemed to happen with great suddenness, taking me by surprise, but there was the delight of having the house full now and again when you all managed to congregate from university, or from work and listening as you chatted, the serious discussions - how much wiser you all seemed to be, and more adventurous than I ever was when I was young, it gave me great satisfaction, and listening to all the technical stuff when you were, as usual really, all on the same wavelength, though it was out of my league. Then the hilarity that grew out of the adventures everyone had, and later when grandchildren came along, and we all played at their level again, and none of us seemed to have grown up at all really, and I was still learning; from you who seem to cope so well with this shrinking world, (so huge when I was young, and yet a friendlier, more familiar place which one felt would never change); and now from the next generation whose lives seem so busy one wonders will they ever have enough time in which to grow, and contemplate, and watch the natural world and benefit from it as we did?

When in the past times were tough, I often thought never mind the world, it's the family that matters. I felt that after a difficult day each of us could come home, close the front door and leaving our troubles outside, find peace, and comfort. As long as we could be kind to each other, be happy together, bolster each other up, tomorrow would be better. I always had the feeling that through thick and thin, we were a team. Which was how we survived so well. Although I certainly worked hard through those years, I gained strength and happiness, from all of you, however little and young you were at the time; and unconscious of my gaze as I watched you, always busy - making a bivouac in the garden out of old branches and ferns, or trying to catch eels in the pond (!!) you were tremendously inventive, and radiated joy. I watched, and re-charged my energies from your laughter, and tried to give you security and stability in return.

Parents can be an awful nuisance, even when one tries hard not to, one still says "Be careful" quite unnecessarily, and occasionally "I was worried" slips out, that is a burden one shouldn't impose, although it is perhaps a clumsy way of saying I love you. I tried from the earliest days not to make the same mistakes that my parents made, and it is extremely hard not to at times, one has to fight that, as one is often caught off guard.

Because I didn't want to fall into the trap of thinking that I owned you because you started life as my darling helpless little babies, I made a vow to each of you when you were born that God had let me have you, and that I would love you with all my heart and care for you to the best of my ability, protect you and give you security, but not direct you or take away your freedom, and that each of you belonged to yourself , your soul was your own. This did not mean neglect, but basically it meant not being unnecessarily bossy, or interfering. My aim was to back you up and help, as unobtrusively as possible, and encourage each of you to follow your own path, and to try out new enthusiasms along the way, even if they didn't last. You led; I followed and never stopped learning.

I don't know if being a parent is an instinct which perhaps we have dulled over the years of civilisation, I know the wonder of having my first child and the love that arrived with you, was natural enough, after that I was all at sea. Sitting up in a hospital bed with John in my arms and "Dr. Spock" in one hand trying to breast-feed you, and apologising, "Poor old baby, I'm sorry I'm so clumsy." You seemed to hold the wisdom of the ages in your tiny being and were a great comfort even then. Paradoxically as you grew older day by day, so you seemed younger, and I thought that you were forgetting all that wisdom as you became a proper baby. I felt as if I were suffering from shock for some time, and completely unprepared to shoulder the responsibility of something so helpless. However, from that time on, my intention was that you should not suffer from the extreme inadequacies of your mother.

The difficult thing about being a parent is not knowing if you are "doing it right" until it's too late, but perhaps if you have respect for the individual, no matter how small that individual is, then possibly you don't go too far wrong. I know I fell from grace many times, mainly when life seemed too difficult for me to cope with, but I never stopped trying to do better, I wanted so badly to be a good parent and not let you down. I also apologised if I was cross, if I felt I'd been wrong I said so and told you I loved you. If one doesn't do this how can one hope that one's children will grow up to be kind parents themselves?

I discovered how easy it is to say "No" and realised that everyone seems to say it far too often - why? Because it's inconvenient if the child does this or that - not a good enough reason, and how frustrating for the child. We too would get frustrated and shout or cry if some great giant said it to us, every time we planned something that did not seem of any great moment to anyone else; either that or we would end up going inside ourselves because there is no point in expressing our feelings. I played at all the ways I could think of to avoid it. Letting you be as free as possible, removing danger and putting out different things to be played with, when you were little. As you got older I learnt to be thinking one step ahead, to offer alternatives to any difficulty that may be on the horizon. Also to jolly well put up with the inconvenience as much as possible whenever it occurred, I never thought of children as second class citizens, your plans were as important to you as mine may have been to me, I felt.

Each one of you has repeatedly and at different times urged me to write this so now at last I must. I think you got the idea many years ago when I started to write some books for children based on the things you did, we were terribly poor and when you were at school, I sat in the car and wrote four little books (the younger ones were only there for the morning, and home was too far away to drive there and back again in the time), then as winter began, the local Methodist church, which opened its doors to anyone and where one could get hot coffee and a biscuit, let me use my portable typewriter in a corner, and type them up, whilst thawing out with my hot drink. Looking back I can't get over their extraordinary kindness, and that of the other people sitting and chatting at the other little tables around me. I read them to you I remember, and then sent them off to a publisher, who sent me a kind letter apologising for not being able to tell me what was wrong with them, and telling me to keep writing. I didn't know that was an unheard-of occurrence, and that I should have polished them up and sent them straight back! I was rather fond of them, but could see that they were probably terribly old-fashioned so put them in a drawer and gave up the idea of writing for children! Ben said when he was a little boy, "If you could write a survival book *that* would be good!" Well, this is a sort of survival book.

I am now going to write this as if it were a story, and give the characters different names, the reason for writing it at all was that when I was alone there were times when I felt very lonely, also some trepidation as I faced the way ahead: that my little family should feel happy and secure was paramount, though I did not feel particularly grown-up myself, so looked in the library for a book that perhaps told the story of someone who had also been through this experience, maybe there would be some tips, but although there were books on every conceivable other thing that you might be going to embark on, I found nothing that filled the bill for me. It was at about this time I met a mother of two children, also recently divorced, I felt very sorry for her, she told me she was going home to her parents because she just couldn't cope. I then remembered reading that C. S. Lewis could not find a book that suited his needs when he was young, and ended up writing them himself. I certainly felt a book on the subject would be like a friendly helping hand, one wouldn't feel quite so alone, so in the end I decided to write one! I didn't get finished though, I was just too busy. So here goes, perhaps this time I shall succeed!

Chapter One

Encounters with Wildlife

The first thing we had to do when we started living on our own, was put the house on the market, and move nearer to the school where John and David were happily settled, and where there was a little nursery school to which Ben, and in due course Kate could go. This was no sudden thing, we were in a recession, and houses were not moving, - neither were we apparently. For a very long time no-one appeared at all, when a couple did come I felt excited, at the adventure of selling the old, and moving to a new house, but then also the sadness of leaving the home we all loved. However, I need not have worried, they liked it but said it was really too big for them! After that viewers were few and far between and life went quietly on and we were able to forget about moving for a while.

School holidays were beginning, so we spent the days going to the woods with a picnic or to the beach. Apparently when one's marriage comes to an end you suffer from shock, even if you instigated the break-up, and

I think I must have been, looking back on it. However we were doing just the right things, having a quiet time visiting our favourite haunts and taking picnics out, even sometimes sitting in the car drinking hot soup and eating sandwiches while waiting for the rain to stop. Then leaping out of the car between showers, to run along the beach and see what the crashing waves were bringing ashore; beach-combing must be in our blood - my uncle would do it with me when I was young, and with his own children, and now I did it with mine, it was great fun. Off would go the boys, enthusiastically rushing hither and thither, laughing and shouting with joy as they searched along the empty wintry beach determinedly followed by Kate, a small figure in red mac and blue boots; occasional peremptory cries of "Wait for me, boys!" would float back to me as Delilah the dachshund and I brought up the rear. Half buried in the great swathes of seaweed, were large wooden planks, bits of orange, yellow and blue plastic, and lengths of blue nylon rope. The three boys aged between seven and four years old at the time dashed from one bit of "treasure" to another and eventually, to my amazement found two large plastic boxes such as greengrocers use, which we took home to grow tomatoes in, Kate who was only two, but definitely not going to be out-done, found a dilapidated broom with a broken handle sticking out of a pile of bits of wood and seaweed, which actually proved very useful in the not too distant future! I collected the bits of broken planks, thinking they'd be good fuel for our fire at night; however they crackled so loudly and spat so alarmingly that I gave up that idea in horror!

Once when we were talking about our useful finds someone told us that walking for miles along the sandy beaches in North Devon he found a Veldtschoen which fitted him so well he took it home and dried it out, next day he went back and found the other one, pronouncing them very comfortable, I believe he wore them for years!

We were so fired up by this great success that we went back pretty frequently. How lucky it was that for the time-being at any rate we were close to a beach from which we got so much pleasure and happiness. The shingly sand forms a large bay, sloping gently down to the water, you can have a good long walk there and it is perfect on wild days for four little things bursting with energy to dash about and let off steam, and there was always the hope of finding more treasure amongst the seaweed, which was in itself exactly what I needed to carry home to enrich my garden soil. Treasure for the boys was a big tyre to bowl along the beach and take home along with a length of frayed and knotted blue nylon rope, and Kate, enthusiastically determined tugged at a piece of metal hawser embedded in a piece of rock, this she doggedly dragged back towards the car. It was absolutely a treasure as far as she was concerned! I hoped fervently she would get sick of this heavy load and abandon it, but no, determination being her middle name, her cheeks glowing, her hair curling in the salt spray, digging her little blue boots firmly into the shingle she pulled and tugged for all she was worth, long after anyone else would have given up. Finally, John very kindly took pity on her and putting it into a large sheet of plastic he found flapping about in the wind nearby managed to drag it back for her, while David and Ben bowled the tyre back to the car. It was of course quite useless, but nevertheless gave her great satisfaction at the time, to have collected something so BIG, and the happiness and contentment felt as we drove home with our booty was beyond price!

I often had to remind myself firmly that the joy the children were getting cost nothing and it was well worth taking everything home for the sake of the happiness it gave them all. Indeed, everyone had a great time bowling the tyre all over the garden which kept them delightedly exercising most of the morning when I was busy, and our neighbour, Mrs. Downs, told me she got a lot of pleasure when she saw them from her kitchen window, they were so inventive in their games she never knew what they would be up to next! It was certainly a great comfort to me to learn that she enjoyed watching them and didn't mind the noise. Eventually, of course there came a dull and rainy day, but John thought of fixing the tyre to a beam in the garage, and turning it into a swing, so he climbed onto the roof of the car, and using the rope I kept in our temperamental mini, ever since the day we had needed a tow; he fixed it up, with everyone else giving helpful instructions as to how far off the ground it should be. I moved the car out of the way and Hey Presto, with the doors open, and fresh air coming in, everyone had something to keep them occupied. And now it was great fun to use when it was raining too hard to go out, and everyone felt like letting off a bit of steam!

It was a wonderful spring that year and we often went to our local woods, we all loved the way the little path, climbing steeply at first led us onward in single file through the trees, away from the high-banked lanes into the depths of the country. In May the bluebells drift down the slope towards you, and the sun beating down through the green of the young beech leaves brings the warm scent of the flowers, rising from the damp earth and moss to nourish your heart and soul, this is a happy place, where there is peace and the only sounds are those of bird-song, and occasionally a distant tractor.

John, who seemed to be able to climb anything almost before he could walk, and being the eldest would dash off to grab the pick of the climbing trees, with David and Ben in hot pursuit and Delilah Dachshund galloping amongst them determined to join in any adventure that her boys had in mind, while Kate would be running hell for leather behind them, calling,

"Wait for me, wait!" and then, as she arrived beneath the tree in which they all reposed, "Help me up, help me up, I want to climb a tree!"

She was always bravely determined to do whatever her brothers did, and like them seemed filled with a joyous spirit of adventure. There they would be swaying about above my head, with the sun shining down through the new spring leaves, surrounded by beech, hazel and chestnut trees, all this and the scent of the warm pine needles from the fir trees rising from beneath my feet , it would have all been pure joy had they only been safely on the ground! Now there was Kate frustrated in her efforts to reach the first branch, demanding to be helped up too and having to be lifted to one of the lower boughs "to keep her happy" - until I could call out that the picnic was ready, and to my great relief down they would safely come.

We had lunch down in the valley, sitting near the stream, watching the water cascading over the rocks, white and foamy, and becoming calmer and slower, and peaty brown, as it wound its way past us with sunlight dappling the water through the leaves. Suddenly we felt very hungry and glad of our sandwiches and hard-boiled eggs, the sun felt really hot, and every now and then a Robin flew from bush to bush, and so we threw our crumbs onto a clear bit of ground, and the friendly little bird pleased us all by companionably sharing our lunch. Afterwards I lay back on the warm ground for a rest, and the children began to explore. Our wood is a wonderfully welcoming place, not dark and overpowering, it has a mix of different trees, and is probably quite narrow, following the stream in the valley, every now and then you can look up and see the sunlit meadows above you on either side. I believe it goes right down all the way to the sea, though it would be too far, I thought, for us. Whatever the weather, it brought the children happiness, and me a kind of healing and contentment. I went and sat on a large flat rock in the middle of the stream, and watched their heads bobbing about amongst the brambles, vanishing behind tree trunks and climbing up the slope as they enthusiastically covered the terrain, it was peaceful here with the water flowing gently by and as I gazed idly into the distance, suddenly a small bird with a white breast alighted on the opposite end of my rock, looked about for a moment, then, before my amazed eyes it simply walked down the sloping end and on under the water!!! Of course it must have been a Dipper, this is what they do, but when you have never seen one before in your life, and it actually happens, it is an astounding, and magical experience.

It seemed as if we were being shown the wonders to be found in the natural world, which, we came to believe, brings more happiness and joy than anything money can buy, indeed we had never come across so much wild life free and undisturbed before, each one of us individually came across something that was new and wonderful that year. One day having climbed the hill to the edge of the wood John, who must have been about seven at that time, came face to face with a fox, and came quickly and quietly back to tell the rest of us.

"What did it do?" Ben asked, excitedly.

"It didn't see me watching it at first, and then suddenly it stood still and looked straight at me, and I was looking at him, but when I tried to move a bit closer, it just trotted off, I don't think it was afraid of me." He told us delightedly, as we all immediately persuaded him to show us where he'd seen it and went with him in case by some miracle it had waited up there, but of course there was no sign, only a trace, we thought, of the wild scent, he'd left among the trees.

We all loved "our" woods, and as it was clearly going to be difficult to make ends meet from now on, the fact that we could collect dead wood for the fire there was a great bonus. It was on one of these wooding expeditions that Ben wandered through the brambles, and as he explained later, nearly trod on a dear little brown bird with bright eyes sitting on her nest among the dead leaves; he was only four years old, but filled with wonder he backed gently away, leaving her in peace. Later taking me firmly by the hand and without a word and with a finger to his lips to show me I must be quiet, he led me back there to show me what he'd found, and so, miraculously it seemed, we stood and gazed at what I assumed to be a hen partridge. Clearly he valued that experience as much as I did, and very kindly shared it with me! So gradually, in this way, peace and calm came into our lives.

It was generally David however, whose love of all living things showed in his huge grey eyes, who noticed anything that was to be seen out in the countryside, he had that natural gift of quietly using his eyes and ears and seeing things in the countryside that other people were quite oblivious to when out and about.

One day just before tea, he came dashing home from walking in the fields, urgency in his every step, I could see from the window, that something was the matter, and went quickly out to meet him.

"Mum, there's a badger in a trap in the hedge."

"Oh no, are you sure?" (Cravenly hoping to be spared this crisis).

"Yes I saw it, it can't move."

My heart failed me, as David looked up

at me with his big grey eyes, he wasn't quite six yet and relied on me to be able to cope, I hoped fervently that I could. The family had once found a cat in a snare or trap of some sort when I was a child, and I knew we would need some kind of implement to deal with it. I called the others to explain why we were going out again before tea, and searched for something to cut the wire, or open the trap, whatever it might be. Of course we had nothing - kitchen scissors was about it - then I remembered a heavy rusty thing like secateurs, or pliers that I had used to bang in nails now and again. Oh where was it? It had left dirty marks... there, at the bottom of the airing cupboard where I had left it to dry after scrubbing it clean!

Hurriedly we all trooped off to the rescue and David tried to retrace his steps, we went on and on across the fields and carefully searched in all the hedges, but there was neither sign nor sound of the badger, it was difficult for him to remember exactly where he had seen it, also he was obviously tired by now after his long walk and the dash home to bring help, but although he was only six there was no thought of giving up, everyone was getting very worried, imagining the poor thing struggling and afraid that we would never find it, and to make matters worse dusk was now falling over the fields, making the hedges loom darkly above us, and hiding the tussocks and general pitfalls that lay in our way. We slowed to a stop and listened intently, the badger must have been lying low listening to our voices, because, suddenly, David saw it lying amongst the undergrowth on top of the bank, practically invisible.

We had to climb up to it, and push forcibly into the base of the hedge to reach it, I was desperately sorry for it, but suddenly had a moment of absolute fear, would it blame me for its predicament, and attack me when I got close enough? John lent me his anorak for protection and I tried to find the wire around its neck. It was horribly difficult, practically impossible to see or find anything to get hold of, and afraid of hurting the poor animal even more, I willed the blunt old pliers to work on the one bit of wire I could feel. The anorak only got in the way so John took it back. Kate and Ben climbed up as far as possible as everyone tried to watch, and we talked reassuringly to the badger, in turn trying to convey to it that we loved it and wanted to help, and it never once made a fierce move or sound. Suddenly something gave way, and the badger took us completely by surprise, immediately moving off down the other side of the bank and trotting off across the other field. There was nothing more that we could do, I prayed fervently that I had removed the wire completely, and that it would be safe and well. Dusk was falling faster and darker over the fields, the lighthouse across the bay beamed out its friendly light, and stars were beginning to appear above us, as we made our way home talking excitedly about our adventure, and thankful that we had found the badger again, before it got too dark. It was good to arrive back in our warm little house and to settle down to tea in front of our cheerful fire, the children happy over what we had done, and me able to relax at last, over a good strong cup!

After that the days went peacefully by, there seemed to be plenty of sun that Spring and the time flew.

However, in due course, it became necessary to sit down in the evening when everyone was in bed and asleep and look at my financial position and try to take stock of the situation. Working out our expenses in detail it was easy to see our income had nothing in common with them whatsoever. In my innocence I had thought that all we had to do was sell the house, buy something smaller, and invest the residue for the children's future. I had no idea that we were in a recession and couldn't understand why this seemed to be taking such a very long time. What to do? Taking a job seemed out of the question, they needed me at home, I totally rejected the thought of some highly paid job in London and having a nanny, as various people were doing at that time, besides very much doubting my ability to land the sort of job which would keep us and pay for a nanny as well. Anyway I had always wanted to bring up my children myself, it was terribly important to be with them and look after them and watch them grow, better to be poor, if we had to, and all be together, we could still be happy. I was a country person in my heart of hearts and on the whole found towns depressing places. I need to be able to see the sea from time to time, smell it in the air and see green fields, and woods. Maybe the house would soon be sold - meanwhile the plan was to keep all the worries away from the children as much as possible and try and sort something out once they were back at school.

The first thing to be done right away was to cancel the central heating oil and the coal, and then we obtained permission to collect the wood in "our" woods. There were lots of dead branches lying about in the undergrowth, and we learnt to collect only that which had been lying there for a long time, green wood which still had the sap in it was no good at all. At first the children enjoyed the novelty and vied with each other in carrying branches and sacks of smaller pieces back to the car, it wore off in time, but it was a good place for them to play while I sawed bits up, and loaded them into the back of our mini estate. Its an economical way to keep warm, you get hot collecting it, then again sawing it, and again when you have a wonderful roaring fire in the evening. We went a bit mad and couldn't resist buying a whistling kettle and boiled it up for tea on our fire too, which was fun and made me feel we were saving money.

My Mother was worried about us,

"How on earth do you keep warm?"

"Well," said Kate with obvious enjoyment "We play blind man's buff after tea, before we have a lovely hot bath, then we get dry, and have our supper and a story in front of our fire. Then we hop into bed."

When you suddenly become poor you begin a totally new experience, it needs some understanding, you become aware that most people are really rather rich, and have not the slightest comprehension of how one has to live. I was delightedly telling someone about our wooding expeditions, how our heating was now free but hard work. (Not knowing that my saw, being old, was also blunt - it was years before we got a new one that almost seemed to go through the wood like a knife through butter!)

"What you need", he said," is a nice little chain-saw."

"I couldn't possibly afford it." I replied ruefully.

"They don't cost much second-hand." was the encouraging reply, but unless they were handing them out free to the needy it was out of the question so I shut up. However, now and again well-meaning bods: couldn't help dispensing a bit of advice.

"What you want is a nice little trailer on the back of that car!"

And later...

"What you want is a nice little greenhouse."

To start with I yearned for the things I undeniably "wanted" but I couldn't have them. What I really wanted, I decided was a peaceful mind, and that comes free!

It took some working on though, the electricity bill gave me a heavy right to the jaw, and the telephone account landed me one in the solar plexus, and there I was down and floundering again. In the evenings sitting there surrounded by figures, sheets of paper full of sums, bills, and worries, I paid everything and watched my overdraft climb frighteningly. Shakily consulting my Bank Manager I told him my house was on the market and as soon as it was sold everything would be put in order. Here was an unexpected friend and ally, whenever I visited him with a dire problem on my mind he always seemed to have some good advice, or managed to explain things were not as bad as they looked. He was a kind, good man and I always hoped that he would be there one day when my fortune changed. I would very much have liked to share some good news with him for a change. However he retired and banks seemed to become entirely impersonal places after that, and there is no longer any point in visiting them!!!

We were given a book by Richard Mabey "Food for Free", just the thing! Off we went armed with an assortment of gloves and a bucket, the young nettles were just big enough to pick, and had that appetising bright green colour of young leaves, we enthusiastically searched the hedgerows until we managed to fill the bucket, and carried this enormous amount home with high expectations. You can wash them in lots of water like spinach and cook them with the small amount of water that remains on the leaves, but I overdid them and when I lifted the lid of the pan they were not like that at all and there was hardly anything left. It was very disappointing, but we did try again and they're not bad if done carefully and served with butter, they have a fluffy consistency - but you do need a lot. They must be alright, my brother used to be served them once a week at his prep school! It is important though that only the young plants in the early spring should be eaten, being careful to collect here and there, leaving plenty behind for the butterflies to lay their eggs on. We also collected limpets one afternoon for a stew, they had to be washed in a bucket of clean water when we got them home, but as they began to squirm out of their shells in protest, I became revolted and rushed them back to the beach hoping guiltily that they might recover, at any rate we did not try cooking them!

The boys thought fishing was a much better proposition, as they had some old fishing line, which Granny had found in her attic for them once, so the next fine day we drove to the little town where they could cast their lines off the quay. First they all trooped into the fishing tackle shop for bait, this of course took time as there were so many interesting and tempting things to look at, wonderful fishing rods which have a beauty of their own, and were of every conceivable kind and price, they were all different, and I could quite understand why John and David were so enthusiastic about them, and then of course, the reels and lines that went with them. The owner of the shop was not too busy, it was early in the year and not yet crowded everywhere with people on holiday, so responding to their great interest he kindly answered their questions, and explained which rods were for fishing in the sea, which were fly fishing rods; and which lines went with each, he explained the breaking strains, and showed them leaders, flies, hooks, and floats, and wonderful reels for each rod, each one better than the last, and to suit all pockets, he was very kind to them all, and gave them lots of useful tips, so of course from then on there were at least two devotees in the family, and it wasn't long before all four of them became enthusiasts, and regular customers, every penny they were ever given was saved up for various bits of fishing equipment and it was a highlight of our visits to call in and buy something new, according to the amount saved for the purpose! Also of course, I now knew what to give John and David when their birthdays came along! We all trooped off to the quay armed with some maggots as bait, and a few hooks, that being all we could afford just then!

The entire family, settled down to an afternoons exciting fishing, while I had the nerve-wracking job of preventing the two youngest falling in, the water looked deep, black and very cold, and I dared not take my eyes off them. Very soon they landed some small crabs, John very professionally used his as bait, I was a bit squeamish about this, and tried not to look, but admired his ability to do it, and didn't want to detract from his pleasure. Luckily Ben and Kate were quite content with the crabs, they were easy to catch, and looked very good in their buckets! I was amazed by their undiminishing enthusiasm, all of them totally engrossed, for what seemed to me a very long time! John caught some small fishes just a few inches long and I wished for his sake that he could land one big enough to eat, David was catching them too, but it needed patience, and I admired their tenacity and was truly grateful that everyone was having such a good time for the price of a few maggots. By tea-time, however, it was getting distinctly chilly, and banking on them getting a bit peckish by now, I managed to persuade them to return the fishes and crabs to the river to allow them grow a bit bigger. Next time we'd probably do better!

I bought them each a cheap ice-cream, and we sat in a row watching the river flowing into the sheltered area known as the boat-float, and two beautiful white swans shepherding their pale grey family across the water, they had six children to care for. We piled into the mini and went home for tea.

Chapter Two

Self-sufficiency

The original plan to sell the house and buy somewhere nearer the school with enough land to practice "self-sufficiency" on, obviously wasn't going to happen as soon as all that, but as the situation seemed pretty desperate I decided to start with a vegetable garden, in case we were still there to eat our produce when it came up!!

We all talked it over, as we drove home one day. Everyone was enthusiastic.

"Can I sow the beans, Mum?" said John, obviously remembering Granny's rows of spectacular Runners.

"I want to do the lettuces." remarked David.

"No, me, oh alright, I'll sow the carrots then." Ben as usual easy-going and adaptable, avoiding any arguments, to my relief.

"I want to plant too. What can I plant?" demanded Kate.

"You can do the radishes." said Ben kindly, and luckily she was satisfied with that.

It was lovely to have their enthusiasm for the plan, but they didn't know how singularly unsuccessful I had always been with pot-plants, however I had been younger then, with no experience of such things, and putting the thought aside, I was determined that somehow, out in their natural environment, their roots in good earth with the sun and rain to nurture them, our vegetables would succeed a lot better, I had memories of other gardens after all, that made me feel quite hopeful.

Sometimes when I was a little girl, on Nanny's day out, I had been allowed to go down and watch Daisy, my grandfather's gardener working in his potting shed, or follow him as he carried compost in his wheelbarrow up and down the paths. He didn't talk much, but he was patient and kind, and I loved the peace, and the smell of the earth in the potting shed as he deliberately potted things up. There was a different and lovely scent that filled the greenhouses which were very special places, where one was very seldom allowed to go. Occasionally though, he would let me follow him as he went from plant to plant pollinating things with a rabbits tail on a small stick, or watering with a small can with a very long spout; the air in here was warm and damp and smelt of nectarines or flowers, it seemed to me to be the most enchanted and magical place, and the visits were all too short and infrequent. It was a great treat nevertheless, whether in or out of the greenhouse, and my love of gardens stems from then; and every now and again some useful little memory from those days surfaces unexpectedly just when it is needed, and cheers me on. But I didn't know enough about it by any means, so off we all went to the library, and from then on, books on gardening and books on self-sufficiency began to build up around the house, and the more I read the more enthusiastic I became, it was so exciting I could hardly wait to begin. Now all that was needed was a book I could keep to tell me what to do and when. Shortly afterwards the very thing popped up in a second hand book shop, a paper-back, produced during the war years explaining everything and showing you how, step by step, right through the year, funnily enough war-time lore on how to make ends meet and so-on became very useful over the coming years.

As the old potatoes were beginning to sprout under the sink in the kitchen, John suggested we should plant them and see what happened. How delicious it would be to have our own new potatoes, and probably we'd get quite a few from each one.

Up to the neglected garden we went to prepare the ground. The five of us attacked the unforgiving soil to the best of our abilities and strength - it was weedy and like iron. It never seemed like this in books, or in any of the civilised gardens that I ever saw, for that matter. Exhausted and disheartened we trailed back to the house for lunch.

Luckily for us our tiny village had at its heart one of the most wonderful post-office stores; Mr. and Mrs. Phipps had met when they were in the R.A.F. during the war, and had always dreamt of owning such a place one day, once the war was over, so here they were creating a welcoming atmosphere, and stocking just about everything one could possibly need. The two front rooms of their little cottage were a perfect treasure trove, on the left as you went in was a counter surrounded by groceries, the tiny post-office window behind a little cage, opposite. They took it in turns to be in the post-office, or the shop. The other room on the right as you went in had knitting wools, needles, sewing things, rubber hot water bottles, and what Mr. Phipps always termed baldly "knicker-elastic" also old-fashioned washing up mops with wooden handles and proper mop heads. In the summer months there would be some buckets and spades, a ball or two and some skipping ropes for any summer visitors on the way to the beach. It was a wonderful place to pick up the local news too; grumbles were aired, good news shared, and a lot of laughter and helpful advice generally disseminated. Many years later Mrs. Phipps told me of the great pleasure she got out of seeing our dilapidated mini drawing up outside, and suddenly all the children erupting out of every window, and rushing in to tell her all about their most recent adventure, they were always so happy, and full of enthusiasm for whatever it was, and looked forward to sharing the experience with her, whilst I read out my grocery list to Mr. Phipps and watched it all mount up on the counter as he reached in a practiced way amongst his shelves for this and that, occasionally having to stop and think, "Now where did we put that?" Then when it was all collected up and paid for, all I had to do was go and unlock the back of the car! No-one ever had to carry their shopping out whilst he was about, he always kindly insisted on doing it himself. They took it in turns, Mrs. Phipps told me, to amuse the children while I shopped. Mr. Phipps always showed them conjuring tricks and sometimes how to tie knots, and sometimes when there was time he would tell them stories about his life when he was younger. The children loved going there, and Mrs. Phipps always gave them a lovely welcome, she was such an interested listener and they made her laugh. When she was "on duty" she saved up the things they said to recount to Mr. Phipps in the evenings. Here was another valuable oasis from which one came away feeling heartened and ready for the fray again.

On this occasion as we ordered the groceries for the coming week, we told them of our plans for the garden, and the difficulties involved. Amazingly, Mrs. Phipps had heard from one of her young customers that very morning that he had invested in a small cultivator and was hoping to do people's gardens for them. She said she would tell him about us. Feeling much cheered we went off for our walk, John, nearly eight years old, said that he hoped the man would come when they were not at school, as he hoped to have a go with the cultivator.

In the end the young man arrived after term had begun, while I was in the kitchen doing my economical once-a-week bake and the oven was full of cheese flans, cakes and biscuits when he arrived. We went up the garden with the smell of baking wafting after us, I was feeling very embarrassed as I knew I couldn't afford much, but couldn't manage without a bit of help either. When he saw the extent of the problem he looked a bit doubtful.

"Do you think you could do about half of it?" I asked awkwardly, thinking the whole thing was too much hard work, and I was more likely to be able to afford half. "I don't think I can afford more than that anyway."

"Oh, don't you worry about that!" came the reply "Just you leave me to it and I'll see what I can do."

In no time at all it seemed the cultivating man re-appeared in despair. "The ground is just too hard, for my little machine." he said. After all this time I can't remember exactly what the deal was, but I think he was very kind, and said he'd settle for some cakes just out of the oven, and a couple of quid. At any rate when I went up the garden later expecting nothing I was absolutely delighted with what he'd accomplished.

When I told my mother about the hard ground and our hopes for new potatoes, over the 'phone one evening, she told me she had the very thing we needed, and would bring it over on her next visit, I was very surprised when she arrived with an implement exactly like a pick-axe, but John saw the idea at once, and we all trooped up the garden where he wielded it like a pro, and made some wonderful trenches for the potatoes.

When you have small children a lot of chat goes on but wonderful as they are, one does need adult conversation as well, occasionally. I was far too poor to have a social life, so always chatted to adults whenever I had the chance; other parents waiting to pick up their children from school too for example. We were always waiting, there was always something interesting going on, no child was ever in a hurry to leave, so while we possessed our souls in patience, we chatted under the trees in the car-park. It was on one of these days, that one of our pony owning friends hearing of our efforts in the garden, immediately offered me some well-rotted manure - wonderful. Jim and Maria Benson had been new parents at the same time as me, I liked them both very much, the children got on well together too, so over the next few weeks Kate and I happily made several manure collecting forays while the boys were at school, we had lots of help to fill the back of our little mini until I became afraid that its front wheels might leave the ground altogether. "It's amazing how much you can get in a mini!" they said with every sign of continuing their labours, but I begged them gratefully to stop.

After that Kate and I were invited in for some lunch. What bliss to sit peacefully in a warm room with a sherry in ones hand before the meal. I had many occasions to feel grateful to these particular friends, and have happy memories of their help and support, not least in making me feel part of the human race again from time to time, I often felt isolated and as if I had dropped off the world entirely in my icy and threadbare home. I never had any heating until the children came home, in order to save money. However, one kept reasonably warm by working as hard as possible.

At the week-end we all poured out into the garden, we filled buckets from our pile of manure and then started lining the trenches with that, and dragging the earth back over the top. All the old potatoes had obligingly grown even longer shoots, so John very carefully cut them into twos and threes, each piece with its own shoot and gave them to Kate who enjoyed planting them one by one, using a trowel lying down as a spacer between them and then covering them over. John and David sowed peas and beans, and Ben and I tackled the carrots, beetroots and lettuce. This all, in a spirit of hopeful enthusiasm, as I'd never actually done anything of the sort before! As we sowed away I wondered why the whole thing looked so amateur and untidy, then I remembered Daisy in my childhood using a long line with two iron prongs for marking out straight lines of digging, and sowing. Dashing into the house I finally found some pieces of string, which John knotted together and then tied the ends to some stout twigs, we stuck these into the ground, and sowed along the string moving it as we went as it wasn't very long! However, it certainly helped and after that it all looked much better.

We thought we'd started pretty late with our gardening so felt there was no time to waste, that the weather would dash on without us and we'd never be done. Consequently one was always making mistakes because one hadn't had time to read all the rules. Also, I found, you learn something new from each book (Kate and I became quite well known at the library after dropping the boys off at school), as it was never all there under one cover. I soon discovered that we should not have planted the potatoes in manure, but we must have had beginners luck as they all came up, as well as the most tempting carrots you ever saw, and were all absolutely delicious, I had forgotten the wonderful flavour of home-grown food. Every day we learnt something new, marrows looked easy, so we made three heaps of earth mixed with manure and sowed three bush marrow seed in each, I didn't know that you were meant to discard the two weakest on each heap, so all three grew into big healthy looking plants, it was very encouraging. We were amazed at the numbers of courgettes that appeared, and frequently found that some had become large marrows hiding beneath their lovely big leaves.

Having decided to follow my heart and bring the children up myself although we would probably be poor, I hoped to find a cottage with some land, and practice "self-sufficiency" if only we could sell up and move, and also be nearer the children's school. What with spending about two hours of every day travelling there and back, doing much more cooking, and much less buying, and all the other work that running a home with four young children entails, I sometimes felt that nothing more could be fitted in but knew it had to be if I was to achieve my goal. I suppose I was on what one would call today "a learning curve". For most of my life there had always been someone else to do the cooking, cleaning and gardening. Now it was just me! Every morning when I got up, I ached from head to toe and felt as if I hadn't been to bed at all. "Hard work never killed anyone," I quoted to myself, and decided I'd better believe it! Ferrying the children to and from school, so far away took quite a chunk out of the day, and I would dash around doing housework and getting things ready for their supper, before setting off again to bring them home! In the end I left the gardening till the evenings after the children were in bed. As the days grew longer, I would dig, and plant and weed and water until ten o'clock, then I'd stagger indoors in a state of exhaustion to collapse in front of TV eat some supper and see the news, before falling into bed. I would totter around next day to do the shopping, peering from bleary eyes and wondering if I might drop down dead perhaps, and "How well you are looking!" Someone was sure to say!

I decided to try tomatoes. We asked my mother on her next visit to save all her old soup tins, and plastic cartons, we punched holes in the bottoms of the tins with an old tin-opener, and it was fun making holes in the cartons, by heating the poker in the fire and poking it through the ends. John filled a bucket with earth from the garden and we filled them with that, popped a tomato seed in each, watered them with warm water and put them in the airing cupboard covered with a big plastic bag. Every single one came up! This was exciting! I arranged as many as possible on top of the washing machine in the glass covered back porch, which was extra large and doubled as a utility room. It never occurred to me to throw any away so they also covered most of the windowsills indoors as well, and of course eventually large pots were needed for them all, luckily there were some quite cheap ones, at the shop where I bought the seed, only they were soft, theoretically they could be planted in the ground so the plant remained undisturbed and would magically melt away! Although this never happened to mine, they did the trick for the tomatoes when used as normal pots. The smell of tomatoes when you brushed against the leaves was mouth-watering; we could hardly wait for the fruit to appear. They grew so huge; we had to rig up makeshift staging with chairs, boxes and planks. When Mr. Hawkins, the butcher, called as he did weekly, he peered through the foliage with a big grin, saying "It's like a jungle in here, Beef, Lamb or Pork today?"

In fact we had far too many and when they were all about 18 inches high we could hardly move with tomato plants everywhere. We gave away some of them but not enough! Luckily one day someone suggested I might be able to look something out for the White

Elephant stall at the village fete, this was worrying at first, white elephants being in short supply in our neck of the woods. On the other hand, maybe... Hurray! I had something to give indeed. Into the back of the little mini estate went all the tomatoes which couldn't fit into the back porch. Kate and I thought they looked lovely, a travelling forest! We ferried them carefully down to the village, where to our pleasure they were very enthusiastically received. We drove home to a house which now looked remarkably tidy, feeling happy that we had been able to do our bit for the fete, like everyone else…

Chapter Three

House-buyers and Hens

Occasionally we would get a call from one of the house-agents asking if we would be in to show some-one around, the original excitement at seeing a possible buyer had definitely worn off, at first it had been fun and I felt very surprised when they didn't buy the place! It soon appeared that it was too big for the retired couples who came to see it and too far away from towns for younger couples, but on this particular afternoon some people on holiday in the area wanted to see the house right away as they were off home the next day. Somehow it seemed promising, it was the most beautiful summer day and we had planned to go swimming, but I comforted us all with the thought that it wouldn't take long and we would go down to the beach after they'd gone.

As usual the house immediately put on its hang-dog expression, having been perfectly cheerful and bright all morning it now looked depressing and poverty struck. The carpets looked threadbare and suddenly everything appeared grim and comfortless, even the sun seemed to have gone in. How were we to make it look welcoming and saleable in two minutes?

"Quick, John" I urged desperately, "Get the rug out of my bedroom, and put it over the worn patch in the sitting-room!"

"David, if you could dust the mantelpiece, I'll stick the orange tree in front of the fireplace. Kate, fetch the Hoover, darling and Ben take this basket and put all the toys you can see lying around in it and pop it in the play-room."

We all dashed about busily. Things were beginning to look better, the orange tree which we had grown from a pip, looked leafy and exotic, but horrors, the Hoover when plugged in remained inert, switching on and off frantically made no difference.

Panicking, I rammed it back in its cupboard and tore down the drive and rushed next door to our dear neighbour Mrs. Downs, thank goodness she was there, I explained my desperation and although a trifle surprised, she rose to the occasion and lent me hers. I jokingly promised her a commission if her Hoover sold the house, and dashed back home, stopping at the gate just long enough to remove a large notice "THIS HOUSE IS NOT FOR SALE" manufactured very beautifully and placed there by David.

We were just about ready when we heard a car arriving. I hid the second hoover and suggested that the children played out in the garden for a while, feeling that I could probably sell the house better without help, or possible hindrance! John got the point and said there was a new game he'd thought of they could do for a while.

Trying to look welcoming and unflustered I opened the front door. They seemed nice and stood there for a while admiring the view. It was looking lovely, the sea blue and sparkling, about half a mile away, and the heat from the sun making it seem very inviting. Wishing the children and I were on our way down there, I tried to get these people into the house and down to business.

Starting downstairs they were very chatty and seemed to take a great interest in everything, it seemed that we progressed at snail's pace, perhaps this time it would sell. Upstairs I began to wonder if the children were getting bored. No! The hot sun and lack of rain that year had burnt our sloping lawn quite brown and it was very slippery apparently, as all four were happily ski-ing down it on pieces of cardboard which they had attached to their feet. Thankful that they were having a good time, I tried to hurry the pace a little, but next our visitors wanted to see the garden. Somehow these people were not like any of the previous viewers and I wished they would go, so strategically ended the tour outside the front door. More talk, and just as I was about to say I really must go, they asked if they may come in for a moment. Thinking they were about to make an offer, I took them back into the sitting room and offered them a cup of tea. The children's antennae telling them food was on the go, all came trooping in, unfortunately there wasn't much in the cupboard as we were due to do some shopping in the village on the way back from the beach.

John found some home-made lemonade in the fridge, and there were just enough biscuits for one each, while all the grown-ups had some tea and a piece of cake. They just chatted away asking where there were good walks and what the neighbourhood was like, so thinking that they would never make an offer in front of the children I had to ask them all to go out into the garden again. However, no offer was made and when the by now thoroughly unwelcome visitors left I rang the agent who'd sent them. He apologised, and said that one occasionally gets such people who use a house viewing as a pleasant way to spend an afternoon. He'd had a slight suspicion, but as they were leaving for home next day, he thought we'd better see them. I am afraid all further viewers were fairly whisked round and I was pretty fierce with one chap who had a derogatory comment to make about our windows; so much had the iron entered my soul! The people who finally bought the house came back several times to look and by this time I was so bored with the whole thing I think I was just going through the motions entirely mechanically, I could not have been more amazed when they made an offer for the place. However, that was in the future, we still had to keep going where we were, and money worries kept encroaching.

Also, I was concerned about David. Of course he liked it here, we all did. Wonderful surroundings, kind people all about us. Villagers walking past our gate would stop and talk to the children riding their bikes and trikes etc. up and down the drive, and who were only too happy to stop and climb the gate for a chat, "This house is not for sale, no!" I heard him say to somebody, and then there were these notices he put up. I got cold feet too from time to time as well, but had to be sensible. We were at least twenty miles from the school where they were so happy, there was a wonderful nursery school there too for Kate, and I would be only twenty miles instead of forty from my mother. Added to this they would be able to join in all the after-school activities with their friends if only we were not so far away, and we had to find something we could afford to live in, something smaller where we could live more cheaply. So bolstering myself up, I took them all with me on a house-hunting expedition of our own.

Nothing seemed as homey, bright and happy as our own home. However, one we looked at which I thought more depressing than most, was the one David and the others thought we should buy - why? Because a large tree had come down in the garden in a recent gale! They had a wonderful time climbing through its branches while I politely looked at the house. I didn't worry after that, I knew we would find somewhere where we could be happy eventually.

However, we needed money now, so perhaps if we could live on our vegetables when they all came up, that would help a bit, and what about hens? We all thought that would be fun, so next time I saw Mrs Downs working away in her garden next door, I asked her how she would feel about living next door to some hens. She surprised me with her enthusiasm, she had kept them herself during the war and was very fond of them and loved the cosy sound of their happy clucking, so did I, remembering times during the war years when I was about three years old, "helping" my grandmother collect the eggs, sometimes putting a hand under a fluffy hen's front to see if she was sitting on one, and listening to their soft reassuring chirrups, I couldn't think of anything more delightful than having some of our own now, so that was settled. Things were looking up considerably I felt. I bought a copy of the local paper which was full of farming advertisements, horses, cattle and lambs for sale, there must be hens somewhere. I found the column entitled "Poultry", just as well, one would never have known. How surprising it was for someone who had once kept three beloved "Welbars", and expected to find at least plenty of Rhode Island Reds, and White Sussex, (the familiar breeds from my childhood), to encounter only strange formulae like Babcock 380 which sounded more like futuristic androids, than the lovely comfortable hens I'd been looking forward to! Thoroughly put off I waited a week or two, anyway I had to wait for the sale of some jewellery before I could buy the hens. That was a wrench, my grandmother's bracelet, ring and brooch, and also the earrings I had collected over the years, but it seemed the only way to avert disaster for a while and I learned to be thankful for the children's sake that I had it to sell and so from time to time one piece or another went off to be auctioned. The most important thing was to get our heads above water, and in time I hoped to be able to keep them there!

In our garage we had a large wooden crate, and next time we saw our village builders we asked them if they thought that could be turned into a chicken-house, they were sure it could and took it away with them, and in due course I settled on six Kim Browns which didn't sound so outlandish, and apparently did lay lovely brown eggs.

The day arranged for me to collect them turned out to be the day of the school play, and a birthday party to which we had all been invited, this would mean a bit of organising. Luckily Kate would be able to spend the morning at the nursery school which we visited once a week for her benefit, she was very contented there, it was a super little building, constructed for children with lots of different areas for sand play, story-telling (with lots of books), a dressing up corner and friendly grown-ups all on Christian name terms with the children, she was not at all averse to an extra morning and I was grateful for their help in taking her for an extra day. After leaving the boys at school we arrived at the nursery just as everyone was congregating in the garden, the boys were pushing pedal cars up a slope and then getting in and dashing down it again, "Here's Kate!" one of them shouted excitedly, "Hi, boys!" she called and promptly joined them, she was good with them because of all her older brothers, she knew exactly how to cope and found their games much more fun than playing with dolls, so she always got a great welcome! The builders had promised the hen-house would be in situ by the time I arrived home with the hens, so after dropping everyone off at their various establishments, off I set.

It was early summer, the little mini plunged into a wilderness of country lanes shaded and dark, wonderful cool tunnels, beech, oak and hawthorn meeting each other overhead, the high banks on either side still starred here and there with a late primrose or two, often earlier in the year one would come upon white violets as a special treat, but now drifts of bluebells were everywhere, scenting the air. I enjoyed these occasional moments alone, able to peacefully enjoy the beauty around me. These were favourite places, enchanted, with an indescribable magic, these lanes had been here since packhorse days, the hedgerows were old, in many places the banks incredibly high, as one wended down long steep hills the banks became sheer cliff faces of rock and the lanes narrower than ever, then reaching the bottom of the valley, deep and dark , mossy and mysterious, one had a sense of relief as one began to climb again, up towards the light, here and there sun dappled the way and pink campion took over from the bluebells. I was spellbound and loving it, one lane joined another first left and then right, I'd lost all sense of direction, the journey seemed to go on forever. Sunlight, then shade, winding, then steep... and time was running out. This was worrying suddenly, one can lose ones way amongst these myriad lanes, become convinced one will never see civilization again, and worse will surely never find the hens, and be late for the school play!

Suddenly the little car popped out of the dark tunnel into blinding sun, and there in the middle of nowhere was an old man smiling tolerantly at this suddenly rushed and frantic face

"Why me dear, you'm nearly there, 'tis

only upalong and over the top!"

Panicking a bit, I aimed the car skywards to the top of the hill, over the brow - and there it was, to my relief, a big farm gate, and buildings in the middle of open sunny fields. A tall and pleasant man wandered through the building with me and there to my horror were hundreds of birds crowded together on wire shelves. He collected one here, one there and carrying them upside-down by their feet planted them firmly into the cardboard box I'd brought.

"Oh dear, what a fool I am," I apologised "It's not nearly big enough."

"Never mind, this will do till you get home." Said he, and shoved three hens into a large paper sack.

How glad I was that they were coming home, to what I intended would be a happy life!

As I drove home in total silence, not a cluck escaped them, had they died of fright? I spoke to them all reassuringly, no response, I was anxious to let them out.

When I stopped the car beside the garden gate at last and carried the first contingent up the little path, a gentle murmuring began within the sack. To my delight and relief, there reposing between the hydrangea and the spirea

Anthony Waterer was the neatest little hen-house, its roof sloped from front to back, a large door in front for cleaning and collecting eggs through, and a small entrance for the hens to go in and out at one end. I gently emptied the sackful into their new home and fetched the other three in their box. Hastily giving them a little corn, and their special drinking fountain, I shut the door and left them in peace, telling myself that they were better off than before anyway.

Collecting Kate from nursery school, there was no time to go home again, so we bought a snack at the village shop, and ate it on the grass by a stream, resting till it was time for the boys play that afternoon. I seem to remember it was one written by the children themselves, enormously enjoyed by the audience and cast as well, Ben had written one of the songs, and his friend had put the music to them, or vice versa, anyway I was enchanted by the whole happy affair. So after that off we all went to the party in a very uplifted mood. These were the people who had given us all the wonderful manure - Jim, the father, was very good always, talking to the boys, I felt they needed that sort of companionship as often as possible, and he would often take them skate-boarding (the current craze) whenever he took his own two children off to a rink. He organised games, and everyone had a lovely time, he and John picked sides for some of them, and John being the eldest at home, quite naturally took the lead when needed. "A future leader of men!" said Jim, making me feel very proud of my eldest.

It had been an eventful day all round, and we hadn't been in our house since early morning! Arriving home eventually we found a note on the mat, our builder's daughter, Jill who seemed to run the business, had called round to see the hens were alright and had enough water as it had been such a warm day! Heart-warmed and happy at such kindness we went to bed dreaming of brown eggs!

Next day of course everyone was up bright and early, and wanting to go up immediately and feed the hens. We scavenged round the kitchen for leftovers, John got a huge saucepan out and put them in it with the potato peelings I had saved, and we put that on to boil while I hastily got our breakfast ready. Everyone ate as quickly as they could and chatted excitedly about who would carry what, while John mixed layers mash into the steaming saucepan till everything was an appetising crumbly consistency. Then all four trooped up the garden with chicken food, clean water, and two sorts of grit.

John opened the big door wide and out they came, six engaging Kim Browns. Some a lovely russet brown, others with gold flecked feathers round their necks. We soon learnt that each was quite different from the others. Kate was able to pick one up and talked to it gently whilst lovingly stroking it, and soon we all had a soft and gentle hen cuddled contentedly in our arms! Only one refused to accept any loving advances, and raced round the garden with neck extended, and long legs making huge strides, Ben rocked with laughter and christened it Ostrich on the spot. That bird was always the same, impossible to catch, and I became rather worried that it might be a cockerel after all, however to our relief she laid eggs in the end, though was never cuddly like the others. My mother was amazed by them when she brought the children's cousins over one day and the hens happily submitted to being held and made a fuss of.

We really needed to fence them off from the garden however, and on one of our visits, my mother thought she had some wire-netting at the back of her garden shed, which we could have if we could excavate through and unearth it. (We come from a long line of hoarders I believe, certainly neither my grandmother in her day, nor my mother in hers had ever been known to throw anything away. This could be useful from time to time, though if truth be told they didn't much like parting with any of it either! And one usually had to promise to take great care of anything one wanted and return it very soon, "as one never knows when it might be needed.") However the children had a great time searching, they were still at the age when they were sure that one might find treasure hidden at the back of a dusty shed, or up in Granny's attic on a rainy day! In due course they found a small roll of old chicken wire which we were kindly given and did our best to put it up round the chicken house, but I never really got the hang of fences and after barely glancing at it, the hens flapped their wings wildly and scrabbled with their feet until they were out and then settled down very happily to scratch and forage over the lawn. After seeing how happy and busy they were we decided that we might as well leave them free, so clipped the flight feathers off one wing, and fenced off the vegetables instead! The children adored having them around so everyone was happy. We had a slight problem after a while as they became so tame, that when we were eating our picnic lunch on the lawn as we often did, the hens would unobtrusively get nearer and nearer, until one of them would get close enough to snatch a sandwich from whichever one of us hadn't noticed their approach, they were so good at it that we became reduced to helpless hysterics. Each time we felt sure that it couldn't possibly happen again, but it did of course and eventually ceased to be funny.

None of the hens were in the least afraid of any of us, and we couldn't round them up and shut them in every lunch time. Luckily Delilah did the trick eventually. She was a tiny black dachshund, the runt of her litter, which I'd bought for Ben several years ago when Kate was born, the others were at school, and I felt he'd be pretty bored with a new baby in the house. She and Ben had a special understanding, though she was a family dog too, she seemed to know that Ben belonged more to her. On this occasion there we were at the top of the lawn, with our backs to the wall so to speak, and the hens pretending that they were not really getting closer in front of us. Just as Ostrich stretched out her long neck for Ben's sandwich "Set 'em off!" said he loudly to Delilah. She did! I was amazed, then afraid that she might try and kill one of them, but she only chased them to the end of the lawn, then trotted back to us looking extremely pleased, with her tail at a jaunty angle in the way that dachshunds do, to lie in the middle of the group with her nose chicken-wards and her little brown eyebrows twitching as she lay on guard. That was the end of that problem, and the extraordinary thing was she never chased any of the hens in any other circumstances and was always perfectly safe with them, about the place.

When the very first brown egg appeared, the excitement was immense, everyone wanted to be the one to go up and collect them each day, and each day there were more! I did not realise until later that these were hybrid hens, never having heard of such a thing! Consequently they were phenomenal layers. At first when we got eggs two days running we could hardly believe it, but when we occasionally collected nine eggs in one morning from six hens it was quite incredible. At first they laid them in their house, under the hydrangea, and all round the garden, and we had egg hunts every day so I thought the extra eggs were ones that had been missed, but when I did the collecting myself, I found they frequently laid nine during that year.

They were very happy and contented hens, and rewarded us handsomely. Once I had arranged proper nest boxes lined cosily with straw they obligingly stopped laying astray, I think we had to leave them shut in for a while too till the eggs were safely laid.

I made custard tarts, cakes and puddings, all with extra eggs added. We had lovely brown eggs for breakfast, and egg sandwiches for tea, and still the fridge overflowed. Remembering my mother preserving them in Isinglass during the war, I asked her what she had kept them in. "Oh, you know, said she, "That big old bucket out in the shed!" So luckily for us this huge bucket took up its place in the back porch, under the tomatoes and I was able to buy Isinglass in the little country town, and started saving them up for the winter months. Even so, it was soon full!

Then Mrs. Downs popped her head over the fence one day and asked if we had any to spare, she had run out and the shops were shut. Of course, the very thing, after that we became suppliers of new laid eggs to our neighbours, and even total strangers knocked on our door one day to ask if we could possibly spare them some, and with all this help the hens eventually paid for themselves.

Chapter 4

Summer Drought and Help!

We were so excited when everything started coming up in the garden, we could hardly believe our good fortune. I hadn't thought of staking the runner beans before we actually sowed them, as we learnt to, in the fullness of time, and of course there they were waving about aimlessly. There was nothing for it but to buy some canes, I didn't get terribly long ones, but they were a little taller than me and I hoped for the best! John and David were delighted and said they would do that job after school, and despite my misgivings went up and staked them very professionally. I got a great kick out of the fact that there were various things they seemed instinctively to know how to do better than I, and as I believe one should let them help when they want to, and not waste the chance by saying "No, you're too young" I had my reward many times when seeing one of the children, with some job that I'd handed over rather reluctantly, doing it so well and with such pleasure. After all, children and animals, as well as plants, need warm, loving and accepting surroundings in order to thrive. However the lettuce did not come up and I couldn't think why. Months later we heard that it was because it was pelleted seed, and the pellets had remained firmly on each seed due to lack of rain, and they were imprisoned inside so never got started! I can't honestly say that the peas did very well either, I used to help pick them when I was little and can remember them looking like a hedge - thick, and covered with lovely pea pods. Yet to this day I have never been able to produce anything like that!

I had rather expected there would be rain now and then, and gradually it dawned on me that it just wasn't happening, the ground was terribly dry and I realised that I would have to water everything if I wanted it to sprout, this hadn't been part of the plan, but it had to be done to get things started. To our great relief, like magic the little plants began to grow and looked green and healthy, the days were warm, and suddenly the summer was upon us, and lo and behold we had a drought! We loved it, that wonderful heat was just the icing on the cake as far as we were concerned, though it seemed wrong to delight in it so, when the grass burned brown all over the countryside and everyone seemed so worried by it; but it suited us, and the garden didn't suffer too much. As day after day went tranquilly by without a cloud on the horizon, and never a hint of rain, we were utterly contented.

We were saving every drop of water for the garden in the bath. It was hard to ferry it from there in buckets each evening before the children's bath-time, and of course however hard we tried it still seemed to splash all over the place. We went down to the beach after tea when the holiday-makers had gone, to see if there was any nice seaweed lying about, and when there was we collected it up and took it home to be carefully arranged around the base of various plants as a mulch, to save on the watering, but even so, I finally decided that we really had to have a rainwater butt outside the backdoor to collect it in, I only hoped it wouldn't be too expensive for us. When the weekend arrived we packed ourselves and Delilah dachshund into the mini and set off for one of those big stores which in this part of the world always seem to lie out in the sticks somewhere, and offer enormous bargains and discounts on everything you buy. First we bought all the groceries for that week and then wandered off to the gardening department, where they had a lot of depressingly small water butts at what seemed large prices. Finally explaining to the salesman what we needed, we were told regretfully that he only had one big barrel and that was damaged! He showed it to us, it was huge, and hideous and also cheap as the lid had gone, so to his surprise we were absolutely delighted and were able to buy it for less than the small ones, what a bargain! Of course both Ben and Kate being the smallest wanted to be the one to take it to the car! So they took it in turns, it was very light of course being plastic, and looked very funny wobbling along rather unsteadily ahead of us, people stopped to watch their progress with broad grins, and of course they were delighted to be the ones to carry this important object through the checkout!

Well, it is amazing what you can get into a mini, but we had filled the back with the weekly groceries, and for a few minutes we were daunted. Delilah sat in the back amidst the children, who all squashed up in the hope that we could get the barrel into the front seat, or behind it; but it just would not fit.

"I wonder", I said doubtfully, "If we could remove the front seat".

Out they all poured again to see what

could be done. John and David worked away with penknives, and I was beginning to feel rather frantic, and desperate not to have to give up our super bargain. Then Delilah trotted off to make friends with some people in a nearby car.

Looking up to see where she had come from they seemed amused by the whole proceedings, and as the driver wandered over to us I clutched at this straw, a man might know if it could be done or not.

"Is it possible, do you think to remove the seat, and if we do would we ever get it back on again?"

"I think you might just possibly," he said, "Wait a minute!" and returning to his car he very kindly produced a whole case of gleaming spanners.

"They've never been used, "he laughed, "I've only just bought them, but they should do the job alright."

They did - we stood the barrel up filled it with our groceries, laid the seat on its side beside it, squashed everyone in the back except me, and waving goodbye to our friends in need, drove triumphantly home, mission accomplished.

From that moment on, every drop of water was stored in our new barrel just outside the backdoor, ready to be carried up the garden in the evenings. The plants didn't seem to mind that it was rather soapy, and everything seemed to flourish. By pure chance we had grown Runner Beans called "Sunset", simply because I had been enchanted by the picture on the packet, pink and white flowers instead of the usual red, these I learnt later do well in a drought. I thought they might need rain to set seed, so watered each week, holding the can as high as I could manage to create the same effect, tiring, but worth it as we were about the only people we knew who had a good crop that year which I felt was a great feather in our caps.

Having learnt to put my worries on one side for the time being, and now that the hens and vegetables needed nothing more than watering in the evenings, and being fed regularly respectively, I felt we could relax for a bit and enjoy the miraculous weather.

The children would be happy to go to the beach and swim whatever the weather, but I am a coward and want it to be baking hot first. However, it was bliss to lie on the shore and do nothing while they splashed about in and out of the sea. Of course I stayed close to them, on guard so to speak, and as in those days I never seemed to know if the tide was going in or out, one was always having to move everything up or down the beach, generally it would be in the nick of time, if the tide was coming in, and once we had to watch as our beach ball bobbed tantalisingly away to be lost forever in front of our unbelieving eyes. When I finally learnt that one could buy a Tide Table at the village shop, or any newsagent, it meant one could time ones visits accordingly!

Whenever it was too hot even for me, I would try to slip unobtrusively into the water, to avoid the inadvertent splashing of excited children, and take my time about it, but I had no luck with this, someone always noticed and the following scene would be enacted.

"Mum is going in!" someone bellows. Down the beach they all rush kindly shrieking encouragement, and promising they will be with me in a jiffy. They obviously think I need a lot of support and far from my hopes of being able to edge in unnoticed, inch by agonising inch, I feel I now have the attention of everyone within earshot. I turn my back on the curious eyes and inch by inch, like a man to the gallows, finally take the plunge. It is lovely! The sea is sparkling and clear as glass, the wonderfully coloured pebbles below are magnified by the water, and now that I am safely launched, I welcome the company, as the children swim alongside me and dive below like little porpoises.

Lazily side stroking along, my back towards the beach and envying the children's easy and natural movements below me, I am thankful that I took them to a swimming pool when they were very young. It was a natural progression from playing in their bath and paddling pool, they all had those inflatable arm bands and never having had any fear preferred to use their own natural strokes; having virtually taught themselves, John and David were swimming under the water like fishes from an early age, to my amazement and admiration. Ben, is a thoughtful, laid-back person, not to be rushed into something, just because the others are doing it, he will think it over for himself, and then decide, so when very young, he announced he wouldn't go in, I said that was fine and we could sit on the grass and read whilst the others swam, after all it was supposed to be fun, I did nothing to change his mind and read to him happily, and then just before everyone came out of the pool he said he'd like a swim, so we put on his arm bands and in he went, totally happy in the water from then on. There was no stopping Kate, however, she put on her arm-bands, and before she was quite two, would take a running jump into the pool after her brothers, where I waited anxiously to catch her, to my dismay under she went, but bobbed up smiling to do it again!

Eventually we return to the beach after everyone has swum through my legs and raced me along the shore. Delilah has been guarding the towels, and helps to dry everyone, busily licking the salt water off our legs with her warm little tongue. Kate has to have a biscuit to warm her up, this makes us all feel hungry, so we unpack our picnic lunch, everyone is ravenous now, but Delilah is carefully given a few titbits and a nice drink of water from her own bottle and saucer, before we eat ours. The sun is hot and makes me feel sleepy, so after lunch I lie back for a snooze, and Ben and Kate collect coloured pebbles while John and David dig a big hole where it is fairly sandy.

"Don't wake Mum," they tell each other, as they dash busily back and forth. I am enormously touched and constantly heartened by such incidences of their unexpected thoughtfulness, and kindness to me. In honour bound I must soon "wake up" and have a game with them before we go home. John has brought a ball to the beach, they would do better without me, I can't catch and my throwing isn't too great either, but they throw gentle ones at me to teach me how to do it like they do, with disastrous results. We all become helpless with laughter as John rescues it from the sea, or it vanishes over a pebble ridge with Delilah being urged to "Seek" and "Fetch!" She gets very excited and runs about tail wagging and snuffling away, unfortunately it isn't the ball she is looking for at all, but an old bit of rotting fish which she naturally rolls in delightedly before we can stop her! Never mind, David finds the ball and we pack up everything and head for home. Delilah has to be washed straight away and Ben dries her with an old towel while I get the tea and everyone watches children's hour on T.V.

One day when everyone was trying to catch fish, and I was lying back on my towel, I noticed a pigeon wandering about among the vegetation at the top of the beach. Occasionally it gave a little flutter if anyone passing went too close, but it didn't actually fly very much, and was still there after we packed up and made our way back to the car. We were worried, we couldn't just leave it, "Let's put our things in the car and then, if it's still there when we drive by, we'll try and catch it!" I suggested, hoping it might not be, but of course it was.

I stopped the car and John and David brought their bathing towels to throw over it if necessary. Ben and Kate helped to form a circle around it, and we slowly tried to capture it, thinking it a forlorn hope, but to everyone's total astonishment it allowed me to walk up to it and pick it up! It seemed relieved, and Kate held it wrapped in a towel as I drove the short distance home. In the rafters of the garage was a cage, like a long box with small square mesh at one end and a door at the other, John jammed a log across inside for the pigeon to roost on, and we gave it a deep pot of water and some chicken corn, and some porridge oats for the time being. It seemed terribly thin, and was very thirsty. It also had a ring on its leg so we decided it must be an exhausted and possibly lost, racing pigeon.

Next day I rang a vet who told me where I could get special pigeon mix, so at least we were sure we were doing the right thing as regards feeding. When the children told them in the post-office about this new addition to the family, someone told us not to keep it too long or it would forget its way home! It certainly seemed very content and didn't appear to mind us taking it in turns to feed it. I really didn't want a pigeon for life though. Eventually it seemed fatter and looked to me to be in the peak of condition, not like the poor tired thing we had found a few weeks previously. “We’d better take it back to the beach, this morning.” I said one day. There was a chorus of protest “Can’t we keep it?” said Kate. “I think we ought to let it go back to its owner.” I said, and after everyone had talked it over it was agreed, that that was the right thing to do. After we and the pigeon had had our breakfasts we wrapped it up in a towel again and set off. As I was the tallest I held the bird in my hands and gently threw it up into the air, it flew well, circled and made a bee-line in the direction from which we had come, what a coincidence, perhaps it belonged to someone in the village.

We had a swim and went home for lunch - but the pigeon had got there first!

We had to harden our hearts and try again, so after a few days we went to visit Granny and spend the day with her. It was a forty mile drive, right out in the country and much higher than we were above sea-level, we decided to let it go again on the way. This time we put the cage in the back of the car with a cloth over it so at least it couldn’t see where we were going. When we were nearly there, we stopped the car and lifted the pigeon out. This time it was different, I held the bird high above my head, regretting that in the distance we could see the coastline far below us, and hoping the pigeon wouldn't notice. Suddenly, as I held it as high as I could it stiffened and appeared to take an intelligent interest, I threw it up as before, and it circled several times above us, as we watched, it appeared to be getting its bearings and then with a kind of certainty in its manner it flew Northeast. This time we felt sure it was going home, I hoped they would be pleased to see it, and would perhaps guess someone had been caring for it for a while.

We made our way to my mother's house, everyone eager to tell her of the latest news. "I hope it's not waiting for you when you get home!!" she said, laughing. We were able to ring her that evening and tell her it was not.

Living where we were, meant we could have a holiday without leaving home, I never ceased to be grateful for the good times we had which cost us nothing. However my money worries still lay there in the background, ready to raise their ugly heads once the children were in bed. They had to wait however, at the moment there was not much I could do about them. Meanwhile we tried to live as cheaply as possible. We began to harvest our own vegetables. I carefully dug the new potatoes for the children to collect, everyone wanted to pick them out of the earth as I lifted the first plant, like magic there they lay amongst the roots, all the children feeling carefully round determined not to miss one, can there be any happiness like it I wondered, as Kate picked a big bunch of mint to cook them with, home grown vegetables are by far the best. The carrots too were delicious, the tiny thinnings scrubbed and served with butter had a flavour out of this world, and as for the beans and tomatoes when they came along in due course, and also the amazing courgettes! Well you have to grow your own to appreciate how they are meant to taste!

After putting the children to bed in the evening, I would go up to pick the beans, the wonderful scent from the jasmine on the fence would waft across on the gentle warm summer breeze and in the distance the blue sea sparkled while the sun turned everything rosy as it sank in the West. You have to pick carefully, it is amazing how whole bunches of beans hide themselves amongst the green foliage, there was an unbelievable quantity to harvest, and each evening there were more. I took them into the house and sliced up enough for the next day, then I put as many as would fit into the fridge. Really there were far too many for us. When we told Mrs. Phipps about our tremendous crops she immediately offered to sell some for us. This was encouraging, it was fun seeing our beans, courgettes and tomatoes waiting on the counter, and I was able to buy other things like flour, with the proceeds. We began to try bread-making. I don't think it rose as it should but it didn't seem to matter much. I made little wholemeal rolls, left them to rise over-night and popped them into a hot oven next morning and in fifteen minutes they were ready. The smell wafting over the kitchen was delicious, a wonderful start to the day, eaten with a lovely brown egg each. Summer living is a lot easier somehow, the children run in and out of the house barefoot and in shorts, we picnicked in the garden, the woods or beach and the children thrived, and I was getting an enormous amount of happiness from watching them, and from just enjoying the simple life.

In the beginning though, when we were alone for the first time, I had been very nervous at night. I would bath the children, one after the other and give them supper in front of the fire and read them a bedtime story. Once they were all tucked up for the night I would put on TV just for the comfort of the noise droning on, it was so quiet once they were all in bed. Finally after tidying up and having my own supper, I would watch something on TV for a while, if I didn't have any bills or other horrors to sort out, and go to bed. But not to sleep, no, there I would be listening to every creak and rustle that houses normally produce, until eventually, generally as a comforting dawn broke, I would nod off. I could not go on like this. Of course I "said my prayers" as I had been taught as a child, but it felt like saying them into a void. I needed to know that we were not alone. I had faith, all my life I had tried to have, but now and again somehow it didn't seem enough. One morning when all the children were at school and Kate at nursery, and I was alone in the house, when the most pressing morning chores were done, I went into my bedroom to sit and give some thought to the problem. Sun poured in through the window bringing light and warmth into my cold house, the only blot on the landscape was me, afraid to sleep, terrified of the bills, worried sick about the future of my children, wanting above everything else to do my best for them and give them a secure and happy life. I tried to let the peace around me enter into my heart and mind, I said "Lord I believe, help Thou mine unbelief". The thought of those sleepless nights made me long for a sign that I had been heard, however, as usual there was only silence. Then something I had heard came into my mind, "Give your troubles to God, if you have nothing to give, then give those;" and I knew that I had to give him my fears, to be rid of them. That night I had the best sleep I'd had for ages and from then on until the children were grown up I usually slept like a log.

As time went by and the weather improved, spring came into the garden and along the lanes around our house, the children seemed happy and thriving, I had so much to be grateful for, and yet the difficulties and worries often seemed too much for me, especially in the cold and often bleak days early in the year.

I always watched the programme "Faith for Life" on TV and about this time someone came on one night and said, "God comes to each one of us in a way that that one person can understand," I was still feeling terribly alone and envied the Faith exhibited by those Christians who occasionally come to ones notice, in the News, in books or wherever. They seem to display a wonderful calmness, happiness and confidence. Is it their ability to believe without question or doubt? Does this confidence come from God, or were they in reality born like that? I wondered.

I was determined that my worries would not reach the children, which was why the post went straight into a drawer and was not even glanced at until they were all in bed, when I had to face whatever was there and get my feeling sick, and shakiness at the sight of the bills over with by myself. I used to look at people chatting in the street sometimes and think, they don't look as if they have any more money than we do, how can they possibly laugh, how do they cope. Did their bills not send them into a sick panic? How could they look so calm and capable, content even, I never heard of anyone having to do without heating, or save electricity as I did. It was unbelievably hard to smile at times, and I felt then that it was almost impossible to appear calm and normal. I did not know then that we were below the poverty level, and I had never heard of the benefit system!!!

On this particular night the clergyman on Faith for Life suddenly said, "It is so simple, all you have to do is say "Thy Will be Done", but we hold ourselves back, we cannot do it because we are afraid He will ask too much of us, but he doesn't, He asks from each of us only what we can manage". It was as if he were looking at and talking only to me. It was exactly what I needed, that is exactly what I had been afraid to say, I wanted to bring up my children, I wanted to make them happy and help them grow into well-balanced and fulfilled adults, if possible. I was afraid God always sent people who wished to do his will off to be Missionaries or some other thing which would mean sacrifices I was incapable of. As a child anything that one didn't want to do or was rather afraid of almost always turned out "to be ones duty" , and so I had never actually dared to use those words. I went off to bed greatly comforted and thankful to that Priest, I would have another "Go" at it in the morning.

Again I sat in my room when all was peaceful, the window was open and I could hear bird song in the garden. I thought about what I wanted to ask. I told God about my feeling that my children needed someone, wiser and braver than I to protect them, and how I needed someone in my head to help me deal with the world on their behalf, and in my backbone to help me protect them against the world when necessary. I asked him to help us to be happy. Then I named each child with all my love and asked him to take us all into his care, and to be with us, and said "Thy Will be Done".

I had not known, how it would be, that immediately great joy and happiness flooded my whole being, my room seemed filled even more with the wonderful sunlight, it seemed as if I had never seen it this way before, I blinked and gazed around, and it was wonderful, I wanted to run exultantly through the world, fly onto the roof and sing so that everyone everywhere might share it. It was the most amazing moment of my life and a quite unmistakeable occurrence, nothing like it had ever happened before, nor since. Many years later a friend told me I had had "a religious experience". I only know that from then on I was helped whenever I turned to Him, and in spite of being a pretty inadequate, inefficient "unbrave" individual, that help was always forthcoming no matter how big or how impossible the problem seemed to be.

Chapter Five

Summer Harvest

It was a wonderful summer, it was as if time stood still, every day the sun shone, we were all as brown as berries my mother said when she visited, and there was approval in her voice, we never thought then, the day would come when the sun which gave us so much happiness would pose a danger to our children. We picnicked on the beach or in the woods and enjoyed just being out in it. To this moment I remember those lovely long tranquil days. However as usual by August, in spite of the heat there were hints that summer would soon be on the wane, now and then a sudden coolness in a small breeze that made one shiver involuntarily, a crispness in the early morning, that hinted briefly of Autumn, and then was swiftly dispersed by the fierceness in the sun as it ripened the corn, and the fruits, to sustain us all through the winter months.

I began to think about the fact that the three younger children had never been Christened, and hoped to put this right before the Autumn term began, so one day when our

Vicar called on one of his regular visits to his parishioners ("don't make any tea" he used to beg having been offered it in every house in the village!), I asked him what could be arranged. I remember he told me that a new type of Christening was being introduced, not a private service but ones child being Christened at the end of a normal service in a short ceremony. I was delighted, thinking that would be perfect and would really make my children part of the parish and all the people of the village would be sharing in it. He tactfully pointed out that not everyone would want to stay perhaps, but that he would announce what was about to happen at the end of the service and we would see what happened. He was as pleased as I was and asked me if I realised that we would be the first in our village to have the new service, and then we talked about when and how it would go. I didn't want John to feel left out of it all, and as the others were no longer babies, it was decided that he could present them at the font with his hand on each of their shoulders as they went forward. As the organist would be on holiday at the time Mrs. Downs from next door would play the organ, she was very worried about not being a very good organist she said, specially as I wanted the hymn "He who would true valour see" for my boys, and she was not very sure of it. Personally I would not have minded if she had played with her feet, it was so lovely to have her doing it. We planned it so it would be just the way I think a Christening should be - no pomp and ceremony, Champagne and Christening cake, worldliness; but quiet and gentle, a Holy and comfortable entering into the church and Christian community. My parents and my brother and his wife were to come and the people we loved from our village, apart from Mrs. Downs, there was her husband, and Mr. and Mrs. Phipps from the Post Office, who had become such an important part of our lives and the Vicar and his wife.

Now that was all settled panic set in, the children had nothing to wear but tee shirts and jeans with patches on the knees - what to do? I had given in to temptation and bought "The Lady" earlier in the day, and looked in there for inspiration - there at the back was an advertisement from someone wanting a house for a holiday at the end of the month! Wondering if I had gone mad and not waiting to get cold feet about it I rang and offered them ours, on condition that they fed the chickens and watered the tomatoes! They told me what they were prepared to offer and the deal was clinched. Then I rang my brother who had once offered me a wing of his house should I need it, to my relief they at once said we must go to them, and they would love to have us. So in due course we packed ourselves, our luggage, one garden chair/bed for Kate, assorted pillows and blankets, two budgies, a gerbil and Delilah into the mini and off we went, to have a holiday of our own. We were taken to zoos and museums and so on which were the sort of things we never did at home where our pleasures had to be of the free variety, so it was a great experience for the children. When it was time to go home, they spent a large part of the journey discussing what they would do if they grew up rich like Uncle James! I felt rich though, it was wonderful to receive the cheque upon our arrival home and I was able to go out and clothe each child from top to toe. I would be able to go in my trouser suit, which was the only respectable thing I possessed, the Vicar understood my predicament, and said that anyway as they couldn't afford to heat the church it would be the most suitable thing to wear, now the evenings were getting chillier.

After that we had a busy week, the children were still at an age when it is rather fun to do helpful grownup jobs, and we polished and hoovered and tidied and they were a real help as I cooked Cheese flans and made salads and things for an evening buffet for everyone. This was home, and the children couldn't see what was worrying me, that everywhere was so threadbare and shabby, the carpets worn through to the canvas in places. Then I had a brainwave - we moved all the furniture about and rearranged the room, doing our best to cover the worst bits, Autumn was setting in so we could have a big and cheerful fire in the grate, using the logs we had collected and sawed up through the year. I had a large rug in my room which went at an angle over the worst part of the carpet, and the children's bedroom mats were also dotted around. The orange tree was put in a corner as a focal point and vases of leafy branches and flowers were dotted about too.

As seemed to be usual that year we woke to a sunny day and the house had its happy face on. When the children were dressed for the occasion they looked festive and happy too, I hate to dress children in the drab grey flannel of my childhood and thought God would understand; John had a blue shirt and pullover and blue tweed trousers, he was taking his responsibility for the occasion very seriously, and looked handsome and dependable and very grownup. David had a wonderful autumnal red shirt, which suited his cheerful glowing nature, and brown tweed trousers. His thick dark hair which curled a bit in spite of his efforts to flatten it, and his huge grey eyes with long lashes, his kind nature, and his genuine interest in everyone he met, made everyone warm to him right away, but he was quite unaware of this and was just thoroughly delighted at the thought of everyone coming to supper with us after church that evening. Ben had blue cords with a shirt covered in colourful toy soldiers, he was always even tempered and of a sunny disposition, content with life, and could be relied upon to be easy-going what ever happened around him. He too was looking forward to the festivities, and helped with everyone else to get everything ready. Kate had a mind of her own, and it often required a lot of tact to get her to change it but she had finally reluctantly agreed to wear a long red pinafore skirt down to her toes, with a frilly white shirt and she looked lovely (though she managed to be back in her old trousers with the patches before more than two photographs had been taken later!).

I shall always treasure the moment when they all stood together around the font, it was a loving, happy and holy occasion, and afterwards several people came up and said how glad they had been to be there, and how they had said a prayer for the children, I was very grateful for that and have never forgotten their kindness, I didn't even know their names. The church was a small and simple one in the middle of our small village and that day it seemed to me to be full of happiness and love. I prayed that the essence of that occasion would somehow remain in our hearts throughout our lives.

Then it was home for a meal altogether, and the little house welcomed us in, and my sister-in-law told my mother, who told me, that she had never seen it looking so lovely!!!!

Next day, the end of the summer holidays, was not exactly warm, and feeling that it might be the last of the summer weather we decided to spend the afternoon on the beach. The wind was rising and we wore warm jerseys for the first time, we found that we had the whole place to ourselves and decided to see if we could get right to the end of the bay and back, the beach was deserted and the waves crashed on the shore as if to signal a new season was beginning, there was a lot of seaweed washed up all fresh and gleaming and slippery, and the boys jumped up and down on the bladderwrack, making it pop in a satisfying way. I looked for shells having once found some small false cowries amongst the pebbles, but in the end there was nothing for it but to join everyone else, running and jumping all over the place, enjoying the way the wind seemed to carry us along, blowing us hither and thither. Delilah her tail well up and ears flapping dashed about with equal enthusiasm. Eventually Kate who was game for anything, and would never give in, showed signs of tiring, and after all the extra mileage we had put in, rushing around in circles and up and down, we decided to make our way homewards. We all took it in turns to give Kate piggy backs, and were feeling pretty hot and tired ourselves, what a long way we had come! As the wind abated and the evening sun turned the whole bay pink, David noticed a big tree trunk in the water just ahead of us, it seemed to be keeping just in front, going at the same speed as we were.

"It's coming in!" shouted John. So off dashed everybody again, keeping pace with this wonderful find, hoping it would come ashore. Obligingly it was not until we were nearly back near the car that the great trunk seemed almost to have grounded. Tantalisingly there was quite an expanse of water between it and the boys! Kate and I were still some way back, and I could see them taking it in turns to dash in after each wave to try and grab a branch and tug it ashore. It was more of a huge log really, with a few little bits of branches at the end, or were they roots? First John got hold of it and gave as big a pull as possible before the next wave, then David, then Ben not to be outdone, did his best too, but was not quite quick enough getting back. Splash, the wave got his legs. Everybody thought this was a great joke, and redoubled their efforts; they had to get it ashore now! The sea was coming in and eventually an obliging wave positioned it just right. Success! One last pull, and there it was, beached. They all promptly leapt upon it, playing follow-my-leader along its length, jumping off just before reaching the sea, and running around for another go, then as the water followed it up the beach they co-ordinated their efforts to roll it with their feet.

"Don't get wet..." they didn't hear me, and my voice tailed off into silence. Why spoil their fun, I was so glad that they found happiness all around them. I watched as they dexterously balanced and ran along one after the other, going a little further, being a bit more daring, until the tide came right up and tipped them all pell-mell into the water! Shrieking with laughter they came running up "Did you see that wave?"

The sea had reclaimed its trophy, and I urged them to race back to the car before they got cold. Then I realised we were not alone, a tallish woman had been watching all the time, and was making her way over to me. Oh dear, I thought I could see disapproval of such disgraceful behaviour written all over her, what could I say, four children fully clad into the sea forsooth! There was no avoiding her - to my surprise and delight she smiled and told me how much she had enjoyed watching them, how lovely it was to see children enjoying themselves and not having to worry about their clothes!! My sentiments exactly, I thought.

I am afraid that from then on every summer holiday seemed to end with everyone falling into the sea, a stream, or some water somewhere; it seemed to become a family tradition! Luckily from our earliest days I had always travelled with spare clothes for everyone - one never knows...

Next day the journey back to school was enlivened by everyone singing at the tops of their voices, how different from my depressed and anxious trips as a child, and how determined I was to keep them there, come what may.

The early mornings now were becoming definitely autumnal, and we began to prepare for winter. Kate went to nursery school only once or twice a week in the early days so she and I took picnic lunches to the woods, then filled the back of the car with as much wood as we could manage. Long branches lay beneath the all enveloping brambles, these we dragged back to the car in ones and twos. Back and fore we went, Kate having a piggy-back on the outward trips and dragging an occasional Kate sized branch back, whilst Delilah dashed about snuffling fiercely into holes beneath trees, and chasing the ends of the branches as we went. By the time we got all that unloaded and stored away at home, it would be time to go and fetch the boys. I hated having to drag her all that way every morning and evening, and it was a long drive for the others too, however there was nothing more to be done until someone came along who wanted our house. I did not understand that there was a recession which was affecting everything.

One morning after taking everyone to school, as a change from wooding and as the sun was shining Kate and I took our lunch and went black-berrying, the best and most prolific bushes lay along the top of the cliffs above "our" beach, now deserted apart from crowds of dainty Black-headed gulls, a few Herring gulls, and one or two Black-backs. We picked and picked, at least I did, Kate collected some in her bucket and then couldn't resist eating them and I had to think of things for her to do to stop her getting bored! Eventually as the gentle September sun shone down we were glad to lie among the scented grasses and refresh ourselves with some lunch. Soon it would be time to fetch the boys from school, but further up the hill I glimpsed an Elderberry tree, so girding up our loins again we went to investigate. Wonderful, it was weighed down with berries and I picked fast and furiously, though careful as always to leave plenty for the birds. It was rather a pity that we had no apples to mix with these fruits, but perhaps one day our new home would have a garden with apple trees in it! That night our small kitchen seemed very crowded with two jelly-bags suspended above the table and two lots of wonderful purple juice dripping from them into a huge old preserving pan lent by my mother, and a large mixing bowl.

The very next day as we got back from school Ben saw Mrs. Downs waving at him over the wall, they had been to visit a large house with an orchard, and had brought us back a basket of windfalls. We were absolutely delighted, that would mean more jelly than ever when mixed with the other two juices, plus some apple jelly for our morning toast as well! I made Elderberry and Blackberry jelly, with apples added for the pectin and Apple jelly too when the children were in bed. I was elated to see all the little pots on my larder shelf, and naturally the children and I took some jelly of each colour over to Mrs. Downs, who immediately suggested that I should sell some of it; so I should not have been surprised when shortly afterwards people started knocking on my door and asking if I could possibly sell them some of my jelly! Consequently I was able to buy some Kilner jars and bottle the tomatoes!

At weekends the children headed off across the fields to collect mushrooms, masses of them came up in the field behind our house, for ages I had been thinking they were stones! When it was time for them to come home I would look out of an upstairs window and see the four colourful little figures, Kate in blue boots and red mac, Ben in red boots and yellow mac, and the other two in blue anoraks with red linings, dashing excitedly all over the field, eventually one of them would see me waving a tea-towel wildly out of the window, and home they would troop all wind-blown, with rosy cheeks and sparkling eyes, all talking like mad and bringing unbelievable quantities of delicious mushrooms. Sometimes when they were in the field they would meet the farmer who would give them what I thought was a very large mangel wurzel to "take home to mother", anyway it was large and delicious, and could be cut up to go in a stew one day, and boiled and mashed with butter another. Often Mrs. Phipps would take her little dog for a walk when the Post Office and shop were shut for lunch, and if she saw them all in the garden, waving and calling "Hullo" to her, she would take them too. Some days they would meet other people from the village walking over the fields, but who-ever it was always stopped for a chat with them, and their kindness in so doing gave me as much joy as they gave the children.

Chapter 6

Grey Clouds and Silver Linings

Occasionally things were very difficult, as the house became more and more threadbare and cold and too awful to invite anyone to visit, one began to realise what it was like to become a prisoner of poverty and to have no hope. This happened when the weather was cold and grey, or when we had nothing but unrelenting rain and dark skies, and I had been sawing up wood for ages and the fire would not light, or some final demand for payment had dropped on the mat, I occasionally longed for a strong reassuring shoulder to lean on, and wondered if there was a danger of falling for someone for the wrong reasons, one needs someone to discuss problems with, to share the burden with, to share all the responsibility with. People got married again far too quickly in my opinion, so decided it was far better to learn to carry my own burdens, and to cope alone, so if I married again it would not spring from a feeling of helpless loneliness. In fact it was absolutely not fair to marry again while the children were little and dependent, better to concentrate on sorting out our money problems, selling the house, and looking for somewhere with a little bit of land so we could practice "self-sufficiency," a subject I had seen a book about in the library.

There was one such cheerless day, I felt abysmally depressed and there was nothing in the house for the children's supper, we had eaten all our eggs except one, (hens cease to produce during the winter months) and as it had been our first venture into growing things I suppose we hadn't produced enough. For some time I had been eating less and less, this certainly affects ones stamina after a while, but couldn't think what to do. There seemed no glimmer of hope. "Oh God," I cried aloud, "there is no-one to help, but you, and it's hardly fair to expect food to suddenly appear!" Black despair weighed me down and would not go away. I prayed for strength of mind to pull myself together, and went to get on with some work.

Against all the odds I began to feel much better, happy in fact, and was able to answer the front door bell with a smile on my face. There on the step was a complete stranger holding out a large cardboard box. "This is for you," he said. Mystified, I peeped in - I saw runner beans, carrots, potatoes and some eggs. "Oh, no," I cried, "It can't be for me, you must have the wrong address." He checked a slightly crumpled bit of paper clutched in his hand. "No, no mistake." He assured me. I couldn't believe it, "Where does it come from?" I asked, in total confusion. "It is the offerings from the Harvest Festival," he told me. "Your name was given to us as someone who could do with it" he said with a smile, pushing it into my hands, and going quickly on his way. Ever afterwards, I hoped that I had thanked him. I was horrified, my Grandfather had been an extremely kind and philanthropic man, my Father had given his life for his country; and here was I their descendant, being nothing but a drag, and having to take instead of giving.

I carried the box into the kitchen, and began to unpack it, there was a chicken all ready to be popped in the oven as well as plenty of vegetables, a loaf of bread and a pot of honey. There were fresh eggs, apples and some butter; in fact there was enough food to tide us over for several days. The relief and joy was enormous, I put the chicken in the oven, with potatoes to roast, and then set off to collect the children from school. Driving through the lanes there was time to think, to try and sort out my confused reactions. As children we'd been taught to think of others, to help, and to serve, to care for those less fortunate. Somehow, I felt terrible to be on the receiving end, it was letting the side down, I had never asked for help in my life.

That was when I learned that sometimes all one can do for others is say thank-you, sincerely and gratefully, as a way of giving something in return. Then it came to me in a blinding flash - my garbled half formed prayer, for food for my children, had been answered.

The wonderful gift would not last forever of course, and something had to be done now, but what?

I hoped that when we sold the house, and moved, our expenses would be less; however we had to live somehow till then. I think it was an advertisement on TV, about people on low incomes not claiming their Benefits that opened my eyes to Social Security. I rang them up, and a smart young man arrived to interview me, it seemed to me that all he saw was a pleasant house, up a short driveway, he never saw the threadbare carpet, nor noticed how cold it was. I felt terrible and told him the house was on the market and I hoped for a little help till then, when I hoped to be able to pay it all back. He went through our income, looked at Bank

Statements and then told me that I would only be entitled to fifty pence on top of what we had! "Hardly worth it, is it? he remarked, I felt so bad about asking at all that I could not bring myself to point out that it was in fact two loaves of bread, which seemed worth it to me.

After that there was nothing for it but to make an appointment to see my helpful Bank Manager again. I called in after leaving the children at school; I was at my wits end by now. He was as kind and reassuring as ever and explained that I could mortgage the house to the bank, which would give us some money in the bank which would be paid back out of the proceeds when I finally sold.

As winter drew in that year, gales buffeted the house and threatened to take off the roof; at night the wind howled so loudly that you could hardly hear the television. I pulled my chair close to the fire, a blanket around me, and Delilah came up beside me as we comforted each other and kept warm. In spite of the fire it was cold and I had never heard a gale like this one, the night seemed filled with menace. Suddenly there was a huge plop, a drip on the carpet behind me, impossible of course, undoubtedly it was outside, after all heavy rain was battering against first one window then another as the wind veered. Plop - unmistakable, and very large and heavy. Unbelievingly going to investigate, another drop got me on the nape of the neck, very wet and cold, that woke me up, definitely not my imagination but at the same time quite impossible. The only thing above was John's bedroom, he would be asleep by this time and there was no water in there. Then the awful thought struck me, was the roof above him intact, or was his room even now awash with wind and rain? I shot up the stairs, and carefully investigated the spot above where I judged the drips below to be - nothing, nor was there any damp or damage anywhere to be found. My relief was great, but back downstairs the carpet was sodden and the plops had changed their tune, and rather frighteningly become quite splashy. Fetching a large bucket from the kitchen and placing it strategically under the drips, Delilah and I took my worries to bed - things would be better in the morning.

They were, and they weren't, the sun was shining so of course right away things didn't seem so bleak, but the bucket to our disbelieving horror was brim full and in danger of spilling over, so we emptied it as carefully as possible, before having breakfast. We drove to school through wet and shiny lanes, leaves and branches were down all over the place, the children looked at the havoc out of the window. "I bet this has brought the chestnuts down too." John said with satisfaction. "I'll meet you in break," said David "and we'll get some to bring home and roast on the fire." "Get some for me!" clamoured the two younger ones, as I rejoiced in their pleasure.

However when our kind builder's daughter Jill, who was, I suppose, a builder herself, came to check out the problem of the night all I had to show her was the brimming bucket in the middle of the living room floor. Again the rain had stopped in the nick of time, leaving no clues as to how it had got in.

This was winter and of course things got colder and windier and wetter, and back came the drips, we were becoming quite desperate and afraid the ceiling would come down when Jill appeared one day, "I've been thinking," said she, "just let me have a look." Sure enough, as she had thought, the wind, being so strong on our hill, had forced the water in through the tiniest crack between the floor above and the sitting-room ceiling, and instead of being faced with a huge bill, the miracle was that she was able to make us all snug and weatherproof very quickly and cheaply!

We put all thoughts of selling the house out of our minds until the spring. Guy Fawkes came and we joined the party at the school, sharing the magic of a sparkling night, stars above us, everyone's breath like smoke in the dark, lit by the huge bonfire, flames flickering high, the scent of the wood, excitement of the fireworks, and in my case pleasure that there were other people to let them off and take charge of it all. Later drawing nearer to the fire as it died away, and each child received a lovely hot potato each, to nibble as we wended our way through the dark lanes to our cosy fire in the grate, and bedtime.

Meanwhile, before term ended I was planning Christmas. I had decided to sell most of my books at the second-hand bookshop, and then went around the antique/junk shops selling anything else that we didn't really need, so that I could buy the children presents and make sure that the stockings would be filled. When you are new to it and really need the money it is extraordinarily embarrassing, but I got a little better at it as time went by.

The thing to do was get the present shopping over whilst they were still at school, there was little chance of buying anything secretly once the holidays started. This was great fun, and keeping one's ear to the ground for some weeks helped in getting some idea of what to get for each of them. Stockings could be filled with cheap little things that they might find interesting or amusing such as jokes, tricks and puzzles, and it was such fun looking for something completely new and different, and then there were either paints or crayons, pencils and paper as everyone was always painting or drawing, and there was always an orange, an apple and a banana in the toe to ward off the pangs of hunger before breakfast. There was also always a book for each of them, to encourage them to read more! I loved filling these and wrapping the presents up in the evening in front of the fire when they were all asleep. Having been a child during the war, it was natural to save the wrapping paper each year and use it all again, it was part of the tradition to search for the wrapping paper, the tree decorations etc, packed away and forgotten about for the whole long year!

Once term was over the house was filled with excitement, John announced that Granny had given them some money to spend and they all trooped down to Mrs. Phipps at the Post Office to confer with her on the subject of "a Christmas present for Mum". Years later she told me all about it, she got such pleasure, she said, from their friendly enthusiasm, and the way they included her in their plans. She and her husband were certainly a very important part of our lives and so was Jill the builder, they were all of them friendly, cheerful, and kind. They did us more good than perhaps they ever realised. So whilst enfolded amongst the little houses in that small village, and encouraged by the stalwart presence of those three, and others who performed acts of kindness from time to time, I finally built up the strength and courage to move on, but not quite yet.

After some time spent doing their shopping, and discussing the pros and cons with Mrs. Phipps, home the four children would dash to shut themselves in their rooms. Sometimes a notice would appear - PRIVATE - DO NOT COME IN - and then the scissors and Sellotape vanished, and when they reappeared, I would be told not to look under the bed, or in that drawer and I remembered my own childhood, and the supreme excitement of doing exactly the same thing, and the home-made decorations we made for our nursery which kept us occupied and happy while everyone was busy. I went out and bought some crepe paper and glue and we made the old paper streamers that I had been taught, and paper chains too, which were easier, for the younger members of the family.

We made an economical Christmas pudding so that everyone could stir it and make a wish! I love the old traditions and tried to keep them and hand them on, part of the ribbon that runs through time and links the family, past and present. For that reason many of the decorations on the tree are old and battered, but the memories they hold are part of our history, and every year the string of bells made of papier-mâché, and silver paper go up, as they did for the first time to unanimous acclaim at the end of the second world war, when such things had been unobtainable. There is a fragile blown glass bird, whose even more fragile tail has gone, and still some of the blown glass baubles that seemed so magical when I was three years old. Until recently when it had finally crumbled away, there had been the most hideous fairy you could imagine, stamped out of plaster of Paris, I think, brought to my mother during the war years by our old nanny whose eyesight was failing her, my mother was so touched by this kindness that it had been solemnly placed on top of the tree ever since. That is a part of the whole spirit of Christmas for me, the memories of people who helped to shape it in the past, the traditions they kept going for us, and we keep going for our children, are manifestations of the love, that makes life good and worthwhile. Everyone wrote a letter to Father Christmas, a magical thing to do, but worrying under the circumstances, so I tried to guide this slightly, explaining that he didn't bring big and expensive things, they'd never get down the chimney for one thing. Generally though in those days they didn't have much idea of what they wanted, so I could make helpful suggestions! Once David simply put "Dear Father Christmas, Please bring some presents. Merry Christmas! Love from David XXX"

When we went to the wood to collect bits for the fire, we found Fir cones and Ivy, so brought bunches home to place behind the pictures, and here and there on ledges, and gradually the house began to smell of fir and greenery, and when the fire was lit in the evening, we put chestnuts on to roast, while John and I stood on the chairs to fix the decorations, Ben and Kate chatted excitedly about Father Christmas coming, and David handing up tin-tacks and blue-tack for fixing things, suddenly thought he had heard sleigh bells, and the magic surrounded us and the whole house glowed with it,

Christmas Day always started with everyone bringing their stockings into my bed to open, and somehow the dark and cold merely added to the excitement of rustling paper, the smell of the oranges, and the delight of everyone, opening and demonstrating how this or that worked to the rest of us, and as the dawn appeared round the edges of the curtains, we realised that we were ravenous, and hurried down for breakfast, and for me to put the roast in the oven in good time, before setting off for church. Our Vicar was very good, it was always a very happy occasion, and he always made sure that his congregation was out and on its way home in time to extract its lunch from the oven, even on an ordinary Sunday, so we had no fears on that score.

My mother, who had very generously supplied the turkey, and her neighbour came to us for lunch, and they brought presents and crackers for the table, so lunch was a wonderful celebration which ended just in time for the Queen's Speech, followed by a walk across the fields, before they went home.

Everything had been put on "hold" for the Christmas holiday, but once the children were back at school in the New Year, I would have to give some serious thought as to how we would survive from then on.

Chapter 7
The New Arrival

We would not be able to continue like this for much longer, yet apart from cutting down on expenditure, which I'd already done as far as possible, or finding a buyer there did not seem to be much available in the way of options. The milk bill was a weekly horror, perhaps we should have a cow, but they looked so fierce I didn't think I would ever be able to convince one that I wasn't afraid of it. One heard a lot about the tiny Dexter cattle at that time, perhaps a very small one would be O.K. Remembering that Jim and Maria Benson kept cows I decided to call in and ask for some advice.

"Good Heavens," said Jim, patting his own Charolais giant affectionately, "Dexters can be quite unmanageable, not suitable at all!" Believing him hopelessly biased, at first I was sceptical when he showed disapproval of the idea, "No really," he insisted, "They are not the easy little things that they appear to be, they are quite fierce. You would be better off with an ordinary house-cow!" I gave up that idea forthwith.

"What about a goat?" asked my brother.

"Not likely!" I replied, "I have just read an article about this horned fiend that ate the washing off the line, and charged everyone in sight including its owner, and was completely unmanageable. He laughed, "It depends on how well they have been treated. Actually there is a herd I know and they are all very small and very gentle and sweet. They come when you call them to be milked."

Feeling a bit reassured by this, and as he sounded so fond of them, "Could we think it over?" That would give us time to find out all we could, and what on earth would be the cost of getting one, which was a worrying thought, as if he could read my mind he said he could get me one if I liked, adding that he would like to do that for us if we wanted one, this was so kind that I decided to find out all about goat-keeping as soon as possible.

As usual we all discussed it in the car on the way home from school, there was unanimous approval and delight at the idea, and naturally the next time we went to the post-office, "We are going to get a goat!" David announced. "Well," I qualified, "we will, if we still like the idea after we know a bit more about them."

"I like the idea!" said Kate decidedly. "Let's get it."

We should not have been surprised but we were, none of us had ever seen a goat in England, they just cropped up in stories from time to time, yet Mrs. Phipps knew of someone nearby who had a goat which supplied them with all their milk! "I'm sure they would be very willing to show you Daisy, and tell you anything you want to know." she said. "Let's go and see them, now!" said John. I hesitated, and Mrs. Phipps offered to tell them about us and see if we could go en masse to visit Daisy, at a mutually convenient time. Meanwhile, on our next library visit I looked for books on goats, and found one to take home with me. These visits were an occasion for us, the librarians were so nice and friendly, and with five of us taking our full quota of books each time, there was always a heavy load to be checked in, and another heavy load going out. It was great, like presents on Christmas day!

The goat book was disappointing, very scientific and clearly for people with large herds and acres of land, but as I was wondering how to translate all this down to our level the telephone rang and by great good fortune, it was the owner of Daisy inviting us to go down and visit, "at any time". I told her about the book I had just found, and said "Thank you very much, but it really looks as if we would be biting off more than we can chew and it is not such a good idea after all." However, she would have none of it, she told me that Daisy was there to provide them with their milk and it really was not as complicated as all that. "Why not just come along and see for yourself?" And that is how we found two new friends, whose frequent kindnesses lit our way throughout the years, from then on.

We arranged to visit one Saturday when there was no school as it was important for all the family to see the goat at close quarters, whilst I now had misgivings about the milk, having heard somewhere that it had a very peculiar taste. I didn't mention this to the children, thinking rather foolishly that if this were the case, perhaps they wouldn't notice it! Anyway, it was a very nice way to spend Saturday afternoon I thought as we drove down one of the many lanes near our village. Down into the valley it led us, and through woods to a gateway by a small stream, then we began to climb again until we came upon a white cottage, surrounded and over-grown by trees and flowering shrubs, it seemed to grow out of the hillside, and was half hidden by the greenery. As we left the car, I led the way down small mossy steps set into the bank, and suddenly there we were on a neat lawned plateau in front of the cottage. It was like being part of a fairy story; a place apart from the bustle of everyday life, all we could hear was the sound of the stream below and the song of the birds. Was it real, this enchanted place, did anyone really exist here? I need not have worried, as a kind face appeared at the window, "I didn't hear you arrive - shall we go straight up and see the goats?" John led the way after our hostess, up a narrow track through the garden to the goat house and paddock where Daisy lived with her very fat son, Fred. He had been castrated and lived as a pampered pet and companion to Daisy who would otherwise have been lonely, goats are herd animals and need each other, as do sheep, cows and horses.

They both came out to meet us as we arrived and were immediately surrounded by four enchanted children, all stroking and talking gently, "We can take them for a walk across the fields if you like." their owner offered, "so you can get used to them." John, walked by Daisy and Kate placed herself on the other side, whilst David and Ben got as close as possible to Fred. We were all reassured and delighted by these small and friendly animals who were happy to be stroked and went for a walk with us across the field, as it basked in the evening sun. The whole thing seemed idyllic, just right for goats, their house and field on the side of a hill, up above the cottage. Everything so well hidden by trees and the lie of the land, a secret place to retreat to, a happy place it seemed to me. When we finally said "Goodbye" to the goats, we returned to the cottage where we were given a taste of the dreaded milk, which had no bad flavour at all. Richard and Hilary explained that as long as the milk was cooled quickly after milking, it did not become tainted in any way. They also suggested that I should go and visit the President of the local Goat Society who had a wonderful herd and would certainly be very helpful, and be able to answer all my questions! They thought that if we decided to go ahead and have a goat, it would be wise join the society as members were so friendly and extremely helpful if ever one encountered any difficulty.

I looked at John, David, Ben and Kate, it was pretty obvious that we were destined to become goat-keepers fairly soon.

Kate and I called on the President of the Goat Society one day after leaving the boys at school, I had rung her and found myself talking to a brisk, business-like person, who nevertheless sounded very encouraging and ready to talk to us and show us her herd. When we arrived we found ourselves in a proper farm, and knocking on the door, were promptly ushered into a warm farmhouse kitchen, given mugs of hot milky coffee and immediately immersed in goat-lore. I was delighted to find lots of the Society's publications on the table ready for me to see, and several good books covering everything one could possibly want to know, well illustrated, and making me feel more enthusiastic than ever. We were warned that goats often have a raw deal in life as they are generally supposed to be small and easy, and people think it will be rather like keeping a dog. As nothing could be further from the truth you often see advertisements of small friendly "nanny-goats" and "ideal pets", and yet another poor victim of ignorance is passed along the line to another "good home" which doesn't know what it is in for. It was impressed upon us that too many people thinking it would be nice to have a goat, and not keeping it correctly, ended up finding the whole thing a horrible mistake with a difficult recalcitrant animal, no milk to speak of, and wishing they had never started would then pass it on to someone equally ignorant, so the poor animals situation got steadily worse, often having to be rescued by some knowledgeable goat-keeper, who did not need such an animal in her herd, but took it out of charity. We were all of us determined not to fail in this respect, and to learn all we could before finding a goat of our own.

"Goats are herd animals, dairy animals, not pets!" That was a saying I was to hear many times, and one I quoted too from time to time in the years to come. How lucky we were to have found people who knew what they were talking about, had all the expertise at their fingertips, and in spite of being very busy themselves, never stinted in the time they gave us, and their advice was always there when needed, only a phone call away.

"I expect you'd like to come and see the goats now?" Our hostess smiled at Kate who could hardly wait, and led us out and across the yard and through some sheds to green fields leading down to the valley. There before our eyes were the largest goats we had ever seen, all grazing contentedly behind what seemed an absurdly flimsy electric fence. White ones, black ones, and some wonderful brown ones with roman noses and long, dangly ears. Kate said at once that she liked them best of all, and I thought they were quite delightful too. Our hostess however said decidedly that they were not for the beginner, and we would do better to start with a white Saanen, or a black Alpine. "You should go for a pedigree one as they all eat the same amount, and cost as much to keep, but a pedigree animal will give you far more milk for the outlay, whilst any other poor little goat may only produce a pint, or even half a pint a day." It still escaped my notice that taking up goat-keeping was taking up farming, and that one would certainly need more than one goat! I asked about joining the society, but instead we were lent a whole pile of books and pamphlets to read, "If you still want to go ahead with the venture after reading that, I can make you a member when you bring them back!" So thinking that a sensible idea, we made our way home, there was lots to do before picking the boys up at four o'clock!

As we made our way home through the village after school we met Jill Heath leading her two contented cows home from pasture, she would be sure to have some practical advice. "You could keep it in your garage" she said. Well, it was certainly big enough, but it didn't seem quite right to me. She laughed at my doubtful expression. "We could completely partition off the end where the small door is and make a linhay." she explained. Our whole mini seemed to shake with excitement "Great" "Go on Mum" "Do it Mum" "Yes, lets."

Jill laughed, "Why don't you go home and think about it, and then give us a ring. Don't delay too long though, we have got some time on our hands, and could get started if you want it."

Of course when we got home, there was the tea to get ready, Children's Hour to be watched on TV, the chickens to be safely shut up, before the fox started his rounds, then homework, a game of Blind Man's Buff in the hall, followed by bath-time, supper, story reading and bed. The children's enthusiasm buoyed me up tremendously, but I often found there wasn't a lot of time for sensible thought and decision making! However, studying all the literature was helpful, and I discovered that there is a magic figure at which one begins to make money in a small way without going into goat keeping in a very big and commercial manner. There was advice on every aspect of goat management, feeding and housing, and as I hoped to practice self-sufficiency once we sold the house, I certainly intended to find somewhere with pasture and stabling. It seemed to me that we might begin in a small way and go on from there.

I had a further consultation with my team on the way to school, and rang the builders when I got home.

So of course in no time at all there we were, with the perfect little linhay, with its own door out into the garden and another through into the garage where the straw etc. would have to be stored. There was lots of room left for the children's bikes, trikes, and the mini too. Not to mention the spade, fork, bamboo sticks and all the garden paraphernalia. It was amazing. Just in time, too as the next call from my brother announced that he had acquired a goat! A farmer had rescued it from somewhere, and my brother had found it tied up in the farmyard with the farmer in a hurry to get rid of it, I thought my brother sounded rather strained himself, but he assured me that it was a dear little thing, and not wanting to sound ungrateful I didn't mention pedigrees, or any of my new-found knowledge, just tried hard to accept with enthusiasm, as it was a very generous gift, for Heavens sake. I asked what breed it was, and he said it was a white one. Saanen then, or Saanen type.

"We'll bring it down on Saturday."

"You just have to put down a bale of

straw," Jill had said, "And then add to it daily. You only have to muck out every three weeks or so then." As my sister had kept a pony when we were children, and I had often mucked out, that at least held no terrors for me, and I decided to go and see the local farmer whose field bordered our garden, and ask him about hay and straw. He was very kind and appeared interested in our plans as he loaded two bales of straw into the back of the mini for me, and then climbed up into the hay loft to look out some good hay. He told me the cows would eat anything, but goats needed good quality hay, and told me that I must always smell it, "If it smells good enough to eat," he smiled, "It will be alright, but never get it if it smells musty and unpleasant as that would be very bad for them. Now, if you haven't got any oats yet you will have to go to the Farmers Association for them!"

The very next day after leaving the children at their various establishments, I drove out to the edge of the little town, to a large open area with a huge warehouse full of sacks of feed of various kinds, implements, oiled green jackets, and in fact everything a busy farmer might need, or so it appeared to me, all conveniently under one huge roof! I wondered how it all worked, and then noticed that everyone seemed to go and talk to a man standing behind a counter in the corner when they came in, and then wandered off armed with a piece of paper. So off I went to collect mine, and was asked what I needed today, explaining rather apologetically that I was new to all this, and only needed a sack of oats. I was taken in hand at once, "You'll be needing the crushed oats then," he said when he heard about the goat-keeping, "Take this docket over to George over there, and he'll get them for you, and bring them to your car." George took my docket and asked me to point out my car to him, and as I opened the back, there he was with his trolley loading up a huge sack of oats for me. Once again I hoped fervently that the front wheels would not leave the ground. I wondered if I looked like an amateur, everyone else seemed to have land-rovers, or tractors with trailers and large assortments of purchases, undoubtedly real farmers. I drove my humble mini hastily away.

On Saturday we were all on the qui vive until at long last we heard the van coming up the drive, and were all assembled outside the front door even before it came to a stop. My brother unfolded himself from the driving seat, his young son leapt out, "Stand back!" he said, as he opened the back door, and daintily, with quiet composure out stepped this faery creature - could this tiny thing be our new goat? This sylph like being, pure white, on dainty cloven hooves, who regarded us with a regal air through her amazing long-lashed golden eyes. She had sweptback horns and round her neck a frayed and knotted bit of blue nylon rope hung barbarously. She was not what our recent experiences had led me to expect! Hesitantly she took a step towards us, then another and stretching out her little head towards Kate's welcoming hands, she inspected us each in turn, and our hearts went out to this gentle creature who had, through no fault of her own, fallen on hard times. We felt a fierce desire to protect her from harm, and give her a good life from then on. She seemed to accept us, and seeing our unkempt lawn the little creature lowered her head and made a beeline for the nearest tuft of grass, showing us as she moved the cruel sore circle round her hind leg where the nylon rope had twisted round and bitten in. "Can I lead her?" came the chorus, and Kate was given the honour, leading the little animal up to the end of the lawn where there was a reasonable bit of grazing. John tied her to the clothes line post for the time being, and we stood and gazed! Then the boys went and fetched a bucket of water for her to drink, and as she was obviously hungry we were able to leave her on the lawn for a short while.

"What are you going to call her?" my brother asked, over tea. "Daisy!" everyone replied. So that was that. After we'd had tea we enticed Daisy into her comfy new stable with an armful of hay, and wedged a bucket of clean water in the corner for her. She was in fact a very young goat it appeared and there was no milking to be done at this stage.

That night when my brother had gone, and the children were in bed, worried that she might be hungry and not being quite sure how much hay she should have, I went out to check on her, it was pitch dark, and all I could think of were those horns! "Daisy?" I quavered. "Mare?" she responded in the same key. "Oh, Daisy!" I laughed, reassured. "Mare!" said she, responsively. I put another helping of hay over the half door, and was rewarded with that lovely crunching noise, that comes from contented animals in their stables, that, mingled with the scent of the hay, and the warmth that permeates the place, from that time on has always made me feel, all's right with the world!

Chapter 8

Goat-keepers in Earnest

Next day, not wanting to use that awful nylon rope again, and determined to do all that we could to give Daisy a happy life, we let her loose out into the garden, where she appeared perfectly content - oh, blissful ignorance - she was hungry, and grazed where she liked, flopping down for a rest now and again, outside whichever window was nearest us! She could see us through the glass which was what she wanted, and made her feel like part of the family. Later we decided to go down to the beach where everyone could play, and Daisy could browse amongst the wild herbage, and young brambles along the edge. We didn't want her to forget how to travel in a car, as our usual haunts would provide her with the fresh green-stuff she needed, along with all the dried food we had to buy for her. When we were ready, I fetched one of Delilah's leads to attach to Daisy's collar, and we all smartly approached our mini-estate. Delilah could sit in the back with Ben, David and Kate as it was John's turn to be in front with me, there were no arguments as there sometimes were, they were all quite happy to sit in the back today! In the very back, behind our new dog-guard was a cosy nest of straw for Daisy to lie on. Kate got into the back seat to encourage her and held out a piece of apple, Ben and I one each side led Daisy up to the open back of the car whereupon Daisy planted her feet firmly on the ground and became rooted to the spot. We resorted to pushing and pulling, not exactly wishing to take the goat by the horns, as this causes bruising and is painful, and leads to more resistance of course. I then had a brain-wave, and lifted her two front feet into the car, where-upon her head waved about above the roof looking everywhere except where she should be going, we got that in with the apple, and started lifting her back legs in, only to see her front nimbly returning to square one on the drive! This happened twice, and the children were hysterical with mirth, I too could feel myself succumbing to a state of totally helpless giggling. This would not do, she would know we could never manage her, I thought, so summoning up my last vestiges of self-control "Hup!" I said firmly, and to our utter delight, she "Hupped", and in, as though to show she was quite prepared to behave intelligently, if we did! She then flopped down into her nest of straw with a contented sigh and off we went.

At the beach, off went the children as arranged, to where I could keep an eye on them whilst holding Daisy on her lead and letting her browse. We did not realise that she had decided we were her herd now, so her head jerked up and off she galloped like a streak of lightening determined to follow wherever they led. Holding on like grim death availed me nought, I was left with the faithful Delilah, and one dog lead, with its hook completely straightened! Luckily at this time of the year there are only one or two people there wandering along, but one feels a bit conspicuous dashing after four children, one goat, and an enthusiastically barking dachshund as they all stream by shattering the peace and unaware of my efforts to stop them. Daisy catches them up and quite content now that her herd are around her consents to go back up the beach, as long as they do!! This time I loop the lead through her collar, and they creep stealthily away, but it isn't easy, she eats, but if I relax my iron grip for one moment she's off in pursuit again, so I'm pretty glad when it's time to go home.

Life soon settled into its new pattern, we fed and watered Daisy in her linhay then I took the children to school, then after doing most of the housework, I'd let her into the garden when I could be around where she could see me, then off to browse in the woods while I filled the back with ivy for her delectation, then on to collect the children from school. "The village are tickled pink," said Jill, "at Daisy in the back of your mini!"

Once we went to a party and had to leave Daisy in her linhay, we gave her plenty of hay and water, and set off leaving her munching away happily. Later however, she must have felt lonely and decided to try to come and find us, when we arrived home we found she had managed to make a hole in the wall with her horns! If she made a big one it would be disastrous, so now she had to join Delilah, as an inseparable part of the family! Even so, one morning after leaving her contentedly browsing around the garden whilst upstairs making the beds, I looked out of John's bedroom window which overlooked her and there - she wasn't! Horror stricken, I rushed to another window, surely she hadn't got out onto the road? Maybe she was even now happily gorging herself on some neighbours' roses?! No sign.

I tore downstairs, and out onto the drive, where to begin? I glanced into the field of cows which bordered the garden to the North, and there was her diminutive figure surrounded by an inquisitive circle of Red Devons. Oh Help, poor Daisy, she must have thought the pickings in our garden were getting rather thin, and the grass looked greener the other side of the fence, but how on earth had she got in there? And how on earth was I going to save her, but save her I must.

I rushed down the drive, round the corner to the farmers' gate, just in time to see one of the cows stretch out its neck to sniff her. Daisy clearly took exception to the liberty and tittupping (rather archly, I thought,) on all four feet, she put down her head and gave the cow a good wham with her horns. They'll kill her, I thought, tremblingly opening the gate and calling her with all the resolution I could muster. Luckily, for some reason, she decided she would come, and tittupping about in an extremely bossy and showing-off manner she made them stand aside, and trotted home with me. Offering up a prayer of thanks, I popped her into her linhay for safety.

When I told the farmer what had happened, he kindly said "Oh don't you worry about that, let her go if she wants to; it's supposed to be good for cows to have a goat in with them!" She did it a few more times, and I saw her clear the fence with ease, but she was so extraordinarily pert and bossy with the cows, threatening them with her horns, and having no compunction about using them too, that I was afraid of what might happen.

I couldn't keep her in, as she could clear the fence, and even one day, rushing after the children who thought they were stealing away unnoticed to go to the Post Office, I saw her clear a five barred gate with ease, and triumphantly join them. The problem would be solved if she kidded, I thought. Meanwhile whenever we went to the woods she came too, she browsed on the brambles and the ivy, chestnuts and acorns and even crunched up the dead leaves as if they were cornflakes, while we pulled down swathes of ivy hanging from the trees or cut armfuls of young brambles to take home for her. Collecting green-stuff for Daisy became a daily chore, and what she ate changed with the seasons. When we fetched the boys from school, we always went early and let Daisy browse on clean and luscious grass verges, we soon got to know all the best places, and I collected armfuls to take home for her, and of course she munched away in the back as we drove.

She became a well-known character in no time, so it was quite a surprise one day when we came out of the library to find a small crowd round the back of the mini; they were tourists who had supposed her to be a very large dog, till they saw the horns! Of course a pedigree goat would have had these removed by the vet, as a kid, but it is cruel and not always successful to do this to an older animal so it was something we had to live with. Many people impressed upon us how dangerous this could be to the children's eyes, and we were always extremely careful.

This is no way to go in for goat-keeping however, a goat is a herd animal and needs the other members of the herd to thrive, we were just very lucky that our life at that time allowed us to be with her all the time, and when that would have become very difficult she had kidded again and begun to form her own herd! Also of course one could never waft about the countryside these days as we did then, though someone eventually told me I had to have a special book into which I had to enter every move Daisy made in order to be able to show it to "The Authorities". I hastily got one and logged our visits to the woods, beach and various grassy verges, and in due course, more professionally, visits to male goats, in order to breed from her, and continue the milk supply.

"When will we be able to have goat's milk?" asked Ben one day, thinking no doubt that we were losing sight of the purpose of all this.

"When Daisy kids!" John told him.

"But she hasn't any udders!" Said Kate. For a moment I was horrified.

"Yes she has, I looked." David said, reassuringly, and I breathed again. Though, that was indeed a relief, we would have to feed her for a year, before we could take her to a male in the autumn! However, it transpired that Daisy's young life had not been all it should, and it was very lucky for us that she produced a poor little kid later in the spring which did not survive, and we got our milk sooner than expected after all. I had thought she was coming into season, in my ignorance, and when I went out to her in the evening, there was this poor little white kid lying in the straw, and Daisy being totally disinterested. I sat in the straw trying to revive it by rubbing it with a towel. Daisy came to help and licked it a bit but soon gave up, and flopped down in the straw behind me, and leant comfortingly and companionably against me. She must have known better than me that we couldn't save it as she was a very good mother to her other kids, and always knew how to cope.

Milking was very hard to begin with, Jill the builder's daughter came up the first morning to show me what to do. I tied Daisy to the kitchen table with her bucket of oats to munch, and Jill showed me how to put my hands around the teats, in just the right place, and squeeze gently but firmly with ones whole hand, starting with the thumb and forefinger, and then closing the others in succession - no pinching or pulling - keeping ones hands still. It was a very slow process to begin with, and ones hands ached excruciatingly long before the goat was milked out, Daisy was very patient, just as long as the food lasted. Time and again when she had finished and I hadn't she would lift one leg and very deliberately plant it in the milk! So then I had to bring in branches of leaves in the hope of keeping her happy a little longer. Trying to hurry when all ones hands wanted to do was give up, was impossible, it was a slow and painful business as far as I was concerned, and I was sorry for Daisy who obviously expected something more competent in the way of a milkmaid.

In time it became easier, but she was a goat who was sensitive to ones mood, and on the rare occasions that we might be going out in the evening, however hard I tried not to hurry or let her know what was in the wind, sure enough sooner or later she would contrive to upset the container of milk or at least manage to plant one hoof slap in the middle of it, and so delay our departure considerably. I tried every conceivable thing I knew to be relaxed and normal with the milking - but SHE ALWAYS KNEW!!!! We all loved her dearly though and of course forgave her idiosyncrasies.

One day when we were having tea, with Daisy lying on the grassy slope outside window, from where she felt she could keep us all company quite satisfactorily, we made the mistake of opening it as it was such a warm day, so she promptly got up and jumped through it! Then proceeded round the table to see what she could glean! Sometimes we could get away with it, but when she had assuaged her hunger outside and loneliness had set in, in she hopped. Visiting relatives and children thought these great party tricks and fed her biscuits from the table, but I rather felt this should not be encouraged and hoped fervently we would soon find a new home more suited to goat-keeping, and be able to have two goats browsing contentedly in their own domain, before things got too out of hand. Having Daisy as a close member of the family had its problems, but delighted the children thank goodness, and seemed to intrigue and amuse everyone who saw her.

Summer was hurrying upon us again, and thinking we had better sow our vegetables again this year, even if we had to leave it all behind if we sold the house, I had sowed carrots and turnips and placed a kind of tunnel of polythene over the top to keep them warm, as my war-time book said they could go in early under cloches, I then opened it up judiciously and watered inside from time to time, this was February, and in March I put in Broad Beans, and later Peas, but these were not very successful. Daisy's milk yield gradually increased and egg production was good although not being at all business-like I had never worked out the cost of animal feed against yields or anything like that!

Every now and then the young man who worked in the fields behind the house, would lean over the fence and give me a kale plant which he said had been broken off, for Daisy. Also Jill turned up from time to time with a huge bundle of long grass that had been scythed for her. It was so kind of them, Daisy and I appreciated it enormously, and I for one didn't feel quite so alone.

Luckily the children loved their school, and David occasionally went off to spend the night with one of his school friends, John went camping and the younger ones had school picnics to join in, but I felt it would be so much easier for us all if only we could move nearer to it and they could join in the various activities that took place in the evenings. Also it seemed awful when one of them, usually Kate, was unwell, and I had to wrap her up in blankets, and take her lying on the back seat to fetch the others, at those times twenty miles there and back seemed a major undertaking, though she was very good and understanding about it which helped a lot. However, if one was ill generally all succumbed, and they rather liked having their bedclothes transferred to four sun-beds in the sitting-room during the day, in front of the fire, and they could have TV to watch any children's programmes that were on, while I got through the work that had to be done, in between providing lots of drinks and doses of medicine. Doctor Mathias laughed delightedly at the arrangements when he visited them, and left us all in a happy state of mind.

During that summer term David made me a wonderful walking stick in wood-work, which was especially for the blackberry season, as he remembered the difficulty involved last year in reaching the furthest sprays of berries, which seemed absolutely huge compared to those nearest us! It came in very useful a lot sooner, the very next day in fact. The term had ended in lovely weather as usual, and we planned to spend the first day of the holidays on the beach. I had cleaned the house from top to toe, dusting every nook and cranny, and hoovering under all the beds, hoping that it could manage with a "lick and a promise" during the summer! That evening once they were all in bed, I set about doing hard-boiled eggs, and tomato sandwiches etc for tomorrow's picnic. When I finally went up to bed, feeling sleepy, and crossing the bed-room with bare feet, I whammed the little toe of one foot with quite unnecessary force into the leg of the bed, which turned out to be a few inches away from the little dent on the carpet where it normally reposed.

The pain was unbelievable, lying back and telling myself it couldn't be that bad, it must be imagination and was bound to stop soon, I found I could not bear even the sheet to touch it. I took two aspirin and hoped for the best. In four hours I took two more, and rang our doctor's surgery at eight a.m. The relief at finding some-one there was tremendous, though short-lived as I had to explain that I simply couldn't drive in, I could not put that part of my foot on the floor. So that meant I would have to wait until about eleven for the doctor to come to me.

The children came up trumps, David fetched the walking-stick remarking what a good thing it was that he had made it for me, I whole-heartedly agreed as I hopped about and dressed with the aid of the sturdiest stick that I had ever used, and when I came down stairs (by sitting and sliding down) I found my team busy laying the table putting out the cereals, and making the toast, so all I had to do was stand on one leg and make the coffee! John got Daisy in to be milked by leading the way with her bucket of oats, and I managed that by sitting on a chair to do it, (I was an old hand at it by this time!) then he let her out into the garden and got her bucket of clean water organised, David took the hens their food and Ben and Kate did their clean water and brought in the eggs! After that all we had to do was wait. When Dr. Mathias finally arrived I had high hopes that he would be able to put the toe back into place, I was convinced it was dislocated because it was so painful. He had wonderful healing hands, but in spite of all his pulling and manipulations it stubbornly remained where the bed-leg had fixed it! He then announced to my utter horror that he didn't want to give me any more pain, and as it wouldn't budge, I would have to go to the Hospital to have it X-rayed, and they would probably then manipulate it after giving me a local anaesthetic, if it wasn't broken. I implored him to just have one last try, and did my best to help all I could by relaxing as much as possible, but it was no go - hospital it would have to be.

Dr. Mathias said he would make an appointment for me, and left. He had been most kind and sympathetic, but this was the worst possible fix we had been in so far. My mother was away, and here I was with four young children, one goat, one dog, six hens and absolutely helpless. I couldn't leave them all and go off to hospital, indeed from where we were out in the country and miles from the town how could I possibly get there? Finally I rang Jim and Maria, the kind friends who had given us all the manure for the garden, and whose children went to the same school as mine. They lived a good ten or twelve miles from us, but one day Maria and I had been having a chat on the telephone when I happened to mention that an odd hissing noise coming from the kitchen, had when finally located, proved to be an old aerosol can on top of a cupboard, and I was wondering how to tackle it, and she kept saying keep away from it, it may be very dangerous, it seemed a such a ridiculous problem and as the discussion got funnier, I had to ring off as she made me laugh so much. The thing about Maria was that tall, slim and good-looking, she appeared far too fragile to be burdened with problems, but she always rose to the occasion magnificently and two minutes later, I swear, I answered the front door to find her standing on the doorstep armed with a pair of tongs and big leather gloves, and while I'm ashamed to say I collapsed in helpless giggles, she marched into the kitchen grabbed the hapless aerosol with her tongs and ferried it to the top of the garden where we buried it deep in the ground. From then on I felt I could call on her in an emergency.

When my step-father died, in shock and operating on auto-pilot I rang her, her calm voice instantly offering to have the children for the day, some-how steadied me and I knew we would get through, and I could join my mother and the rest of the family for that day, after dropping off the children en route. When I collected them that evening she had already thought ahead, and had made plans for what they would all do on the day of the funeral. Help like this made it possible for me to cope with a traumatic experience, in a way that I had never thought that I could.

Now when Maria answered the phone she immediately said she would come over, Jim was away, but she had an au pair for a while so would bring her over with her children and they would all play at my house, while she drove me over to the hospital. The children were pleased at this, and we immediately began to get ready. Daisy was enticed back to her byre with extra hay, for safety's sake, Kate found my handbag and a coat, and suddenly there was Maria, and her family telling me not to worry everything would be fine. Maria sympathetic and extremely practical whisked me off in her comfortable car, even fetching a wheel chair for me when we got there in spite of my protests. By the time my foot was seen, then ex-rayed, then injected and manipulated I was extremely relieved to feel it going back into place. It was lovely to have Maria to ferry me back home again and feel that the worst was over, tomorrow was a new day, and the rest of the holidays lay ahead.

One or two sets of viewers came to see the house, but one expects that when the weather improves, and we showed them around quite quickly and forgot about them right away. We spent long days on the beach, sold our marrows, onions and tomatoes, as before. John had a good birthday party with several friends, and Jim and Maria and their children came over too, we all had a good time, and with our minds in holiday mode scarcely noticed when next day back came one set of viewers, they said they had really wanted another look. We were packing up the fishing gear, and let them have a wander round inside and out on their own; when they left we waved them "Goodbye" and went fishing off the beach for the rest of the morning, completely unaware that this was a portentous day.

Daisy seemed contented to stay in her linhay after milking with her oats and an armful of greens, but in the afternoon we would have to take her out for some browsing, so that afternoon we took her to the woods and I collected ivy for her, while the rest of the family paddled about in the stream in their bathing suits, and she browsed on the brambles, and Delilah dashed about happily between us all. We had to tie Daisy to a tree stump while we had tea, as there was no way we could have a sandwich in peace once she noticed what we were doing! When it was time to go home, I led Daisy as she was incredibly strong if she decided to dash up the road or do something else on the spur of the moment. We also had the picnic things, swimmers and armfuls of ivy to transport. We got Daisy into the back with her ivy under her chin and she contentedly munched as our little mini trundled home.

Our summer went happily by, slightly busier than before since Daisy had joined us, and before we knew it the trees above the beach were laden with elderberries, my neighbour swapped windfalls for some tomatoes, and it was jelly-making time again, and as all the little pots began to fill the shelves, the telephone rang and the house-agent said that he had received an offer for the house! We were all astounded. We had practically forgotten about selling, the odd viewer had become a fact of life, coming and then going and hardly being noticed by us at all. But no-one's been here I told him in stupefaction, "Yes," he responded, "They came twice!"

Rather like having an injection, anticipating and anticipating, and then it happens and you hardly notice it at all. We were all rather shocked, especially as we had given up house-hunting on our own account. It seemed pointless as every house we had seen eventually went to someone else.

Now there seemed to be nothing on the market that was in the least suitable, our price had come tumbling down over this period, and although everything else must have suffered the same fate, there was nothing about that I could afford that did not depress me on sight. However I felt we had no choice, but to accept this offer and try to move closer to the school. This was a problem, until to my total amazement when waiting, as usual for the children to come out of school, one of the parents with whom I chatted whilst we waited offered us her little bungalow pro tem. I was so surprised that I refused at once, it was so kind, but so impractical, winter was upon us and the chance of finding somewhere of our own at this time of year seemed pretty remote. I had never heard of anyone doing such a thing, we would be living at pretty close quarters and didn't know each other at all. It could be a recipe for disaster. However, she was so sure and smiled at me so kindly, telling me that it was in the garden, not too close and I mustn't miss this chance of a sale after we had waited so long. "Oh this is madness; I couldn't afford to rent your bungalow anyway!" I blurted out. "Oh no, of course not, we wouldn't charge you!" came the reply. "Go and think about it, and come over and see it, before you decide."

I was in turmoil, but in the end we did just that, the general concensus of opinion was that we should and we did! There was of course so much to be done and little time to do it. I think it was the local butcher who kindly despatched the chickens for me, and they were deep-frozen until needed. I was very green about all this and pretty tough old boilers they turned out to be in the end! Jill lent Daisy her site hut which she erected in the field adjoining the little bungalow, Jim and Maria took the children for the day so I could finish off the house with the removal men, and at the last minute Mrs. Downs came over from next door with a small basket in which reposed a thermos flask of tea, a bottle of milk, a packet of biscuits and her wonderful date and walnut loaf, all sliced and buttered so we should have some tea when we got in! This was the last of my goodbyes, though I should be bringing the basket back in due course, and bless her heart it made leaving the house a little easier too. I turned my little mini out into the lane, and didn't look back.

Chapter 9

Our New Home

Everyone was so very, very kind, but there is something horribly strange about having no home of your own, you feel like a displaced person, lose your identity, you are marking time, you feel lonely, insecure as if you were on quick-sand which you are, or we were, as foolishly I put our furniture into store - it was not worth it - and the capital from the sale was just being eaten up. It took ages to find somewhere that I could afford that did not require work done on it, or money spent on it. I felt we were in an appalling situation, and eventually moved in with my mother. At night the children added the request at the end of their prayers that we should find a house, and it became a list. "Please help us to find a house with five rooms, (I thought they meant bedrooms, though on reflection that would have been unrealistic given the state of our finances), a large garden with a stream, a house for Daisy, a garage and a greenhouse!" The list had grown over the nights. I wasn't sure what to say about this, we couldn't afford a big house, and I didn't want them to lose their faith, in the end I suggested they add "If it be Thy Will." explaining that for various reasons it might not be possible, but I was sure we would be happy and enjoy the adventure whatever happened.

When you have children and animals LIFE goes on in spite of all difficulties, it was now that Daisy made it quite clear that she wanted a mate. I intended to breed up as much as possible in order to get some good milkers amongst her kids, and checked around to find out where a good pedigree male Saanen {which is what Daisy appeared to be}, was standing at stud, and was relieved to find one not so very far from my mother's house. I rang the owner and told her that Daisy was trying to dash away from us when we took her out, which with her strength and determination was an unnerving experience, and she was also calling out long and piteously from her shed when taken home, this was hard on my mother and her neighbours, not used to such goings-on in their quiet and well-bred neighbourhood, and the situation was becoming rather difficult for all concerned. Mrs. Jenner was clearly used to all of this and asked how long had Daisy been calling, and then agreed that I should take her over to meet a Saanen male of very good pedigree, judging by his string of names, that afternoon.

Daisy seemed to perfectly understand what our errand was and sat calmly in the back of the mini, behind her "goat-guard" apart from the odd plaintive "Mare!" uttered at high pitch and with a tragic little break in the middle; whenever we had to slow down; or stop at "Major Road Ahead" signs, whereupon she showed every sign of getting out and walking unless I got a move on! I got a move on (as much as possible in safety), and was greatly relieved when we arrived without mishap. I was instructed to bring Daisy into the yard where his Lordship her proposed suitor would join us with his owner in attendance. Daisy stood there with her ears pricked interestedly, and in due course a stable door opened and out stepped a very hairy male goat, he had great horns and a long beard, he snorted and trotted excitedly up to Daisy and looked her over with every appearance of pleasure and approval. He was a very handsome beast, with his long flowing white coat and I expected Daisy to be bowled over by his charms, but Daisy played it cool, far too cool to my way of thinking. His Lordship's owner suggested letting Daisy loose for a while, to no avail, she simply gave him the brush-off in no uncertain terms. This was extremely perplexing, now what was I supposed to do? I felt like asking her. Mrs. Jenner however was an old hand, and realising that I was a novice, kindly explained that as Daisy had "gone off the boil", I might like to take something belonging to him home with us, she vanished with her charge into the building and returned with a plastic bag containing some straw smelling strongly of male goat. Put it near her next time she is in season I was told and then bring her back again. So I packed Daisy and her memento, back into the mini, and we headed schoolwards to collect the children.

Oh horrors! I realised that the overpowering smell of male goat was still with us, all over Daisy, and throughout the car. I hadn't realised what we were in for, although my books had taught me that one couldn't keep a male animal unless one had plenty of land (farm-sized that is), as one had to keep a male on his own well away from the herd with his own stable, pasture, and preferably a companion keeping him contented and happy during the long months between the herds visits. Then ideally one kept a change of overalls at least, and left them over there, after visiting him, as the smell is so great it will taint the milk and render it useless! Now I understood why! There was nothing to be done, time was short, so I turned into the school, and parked as far away as possible from the other cars, no chance of getting out for a chat this afternoon, I pretended to be engrossed in the local paper, and hoping that the awful smell was not at that very moment wafting over the whole area, wished fervently that the children would hurry up. All too slowly they dripped up, one by one and "Pee-ooooo" they exclaimed loudly as each one's nostrils was suddenly assailed by the miasma curling its way out of every gap. "Come on, come on, we are in a hurry!" I urged them as they took their time packing in their books and general paraphernalia. "I'm not sitting near Daisy" was the general vote, but we got going at last to my relief, and opened all the windows on the way home to clear the air.

That night was a trifle disturbed, through the mists of sleep I thought I heard a muffled thump and a bang, I dragged myself awake, and checked the children but they were all sleeping peacefully, even my mother who professed to be a light sleeper, was breathing heavily and regularly in her room. If she had not awoken everything must be alright I reasoned, so I went back to bed and pulling the covers over my ears went out like a light, as was entirely usual in those days. Next day being Saturday, normally no-one hurried, - today was different, BANG, BANG, CRASH, the noise came from Daisy's stable, followed not by a plaintive little "Mare", more like a full-blooded roar. We all got up rather quickly. "Did you hear Daisy?" everyone was exclaiming. We had breakfast in seconds, and poured out to view the mayhem. There is an expression about "Climbing the walls", now I know where it comes from. Daisy had apparently taken off and run round and round hers, way above my shoulder height in her frenzy to reach the enticing little bag of Male Scent reposing next door, and I thought undetectably tied up in its plastic bag.

On occasions like this it's amazing how quick one can be, we had to get Daisy back to the male as fast as possible, but I was afraid that she would probably break right through the goat barrier and endeavour to leave the car at every hold up. John already had plans for the day, and Ben was being collected by a friend, Kate however, nothing loth, said she would help, and David kindly said he would too. So with Daisy safely in her nest of straw behind the goat guard, David holding her chain and Kate armed with titbits, to feed her at every cross-roads, we sallied forth. This time all went well, and if she did not come into season again we could expect her to kid in the spring. We must absolutely have a home of our own by then, I thought in rising panic!

Towards the end of the year, an advertisement caught my attention in the local paper, un-enticingly in the small print, it was a semi-detached house, and I imagined that meant lack of privacy and noise through the walls, but it seemed to have a large garden, just the thing for growing your own vegetables, and doing a bit of self-sufficiency it said! First one agent offered it, then another and still it did not sell. Eventually I sent for the particulars, no good I felt, and more than I could afford. Every week it was still there, no-one wanted it, there must be something wrong with it. Then the price dropped a little, I was getting desperate and there seemed to be nothing in our price range that didn't need a lot of work on it, so I went in to see the House-agent after dropping every-one off at school, and saw some more details. The agent said "Could be just the thing for some-one wanting to practice self-sufficiency"! So at long last I went with no enthusiasm at all to see it before picking the children up from school, a few days later. It was a horrible wet wintry day. The house looked neat, but it was on the outskirts of a small town and looked like a town house, which put me off even further. However with time to kill before the children would be ready, I went and rang the doorbell, and as the door swung open and I stepped in, light and warmth surrounded me and the little house welcomed me in! There was a large sitting-room which ran from front to back, a bigger kitchen than we'd had before and three bedrooms, two large and one small. Everywhere there were built-in cupboards with shelves and drawers for storage, and all in perfect order, bright and attractive, and after seeing inside, the owner and I ran up and down the garden in the pouring rain, so I could get an idea of what was there. It was about a quarter of an acre in size, with large vegetable beds, several fruit trees, a very big shed at the end, and a garage with a lean-to greenhouse on one of its walls, bounded on one side by a lane leading down to the garage, and on the other by a small stream. The owners told me that next door was empty most of the time, the absent owners came down only for holidays, and let it occasionally in the summer they were mature people in the main, and they had never suffered from noisy neighbours, this seemed reassuring, and I felt that this was the house for us, but I still needed to get away, and think; as I dashed through the rain to my mini, they called out "By all means bring the children to have a look too!" On the way home I told them all about it. However, it was not until after we had finally acquired it and were safely ensconced that I realised that it was indeed exactly what they had all prayed for, five rooms, a garage, greenhouse, and shed for a goat, all set around what was for us a fairly large garden with a stream running along one side!

We moved in during the holidays just before Christmas, John was now thirteen, and Kate about six, with David and Ben between them, some years since we had first decided on the move! For some reason it was fairly late in the afternoon, luckily our carpets were already laid, but to my astonishment the previous owners were moving out as we arrived, however as it was immediately clear most of our furniture would never fit in, we earmarked a table and chairs, sofa and armchairs for the living room, and directed everything else except the beds of course, straight to the garage. This gave everyone room to manoeuvre and somehow we all managed, and finally after the mandatory cups of tea, we closed the front door and found ourselves, at last, alone in our new house. Luckily my mother had made us one of her very popular fish pies which could be popped in the oven, add some frozen peas, and presto supper! This was a tremendous help and we all dashed about fixing up the beds, happy in the knowledge that food was on the go and would be ready just as soon as we were! Delilah had waited in the mini safely out of the way of all those feet until everyone had gone, now she explored the house with Kate and every appearance of approval, as she snuffled in all the corners and wagged her tail as she checked all the familiar things were there. Everyone was excitedly unpacking and arranging their rooms, John had the smallest one to himself, with a built-in desk and bookshelves, David and Ben were to share one big room and Kate and I the other. I left them to do the finishing touches and went to unearth the curtains, the house felt like a goldfish bowl as so many cars came down the road that passed it, lighting up the rooms with their head-lights as if searching out every nook and cranny within, I felt as if my very soul was laid bare, and unutterably depressed and lonely. It was the main road that did it, a proper one with a white line down the middle and what seemed like an unending procession of cars, even street lights. It was horrible, alien, how I yearned for my peaceful lane, the friendly dark with visible stars and silence. The children must never know, I pushed the feeling away and carried an armful of assorted curtains upstairs, some from our old home, some passed on to me as "Too good to throw away, maybe they'll come in useful one day." Now it was simply a question of would they fit? And miraculously, they did!

Once I had hung the largest we had in the sitting room window between us and the traffic, I felt a bit better, and soon called everyone downstairs to eat. Outside it was cold and dark and sleet was beginning to fall, one end of the living-room was taken up with as yet, unpacked crates and boxes, but the table was laid, the house was warm, and with everyone gathered around the hot food, we had a very cheery first meal in our new home and toasted the future in lemonade shandy as it was a special occasion.

Daisy had remained in my mothers' shed for the night, as she was "drying-out" this meant she gave less and less milk, and one ceased to milk her at all so that she could conserve all her energies for producing and feeding a good healthy kid in the spring we hoped. Tomorrow we would fix up her shed,

fetch hay and straw, and oats and then collect her, but for now it was hot baths all round and a welcome early night in our new little home.

Chapter 10
Settling In

That Spring term we drove to school along icy roads, the grassy verges frozen into solid white spears. Every day as I went down the garden to feed Daisy, the ground was iron hard, every blade of grass, stood upright frozen stiff. You could walk over the lawn and it crunched a little, but not a blade of grass bent under ones weight!! At night walking down to Daisy's house, my breath rose into the air in clouds, and looking up I became aware that away from the street lamps it was dark, we were in a little valley, with a hill above the stream, and looking up I could see the brilliant stars above me. There was Orion above the goat-house keeping me company after the children were in bed, while I went to and fro. My fingers froze, as I painfully struggled to undo the binder twine round the hay bales, and extract an armful to carry down the path, along with her oats and finally a clean bucket of water. My reward came at the sight of her, in her warm nest of straw, contentedly crunching away on the sweet-smelling hay, and then I stood for a peaceful moment in the middle of the garden staring up at the wonderful sparkling sky above me. There opposite Orion, I found the Plough and then Cassiopeia; this delighted me, and was the sum total of my knowledge of what was above my head, apart from feeling sure that the lovely evening star which appeared as dusk fell was possibly Venus. Every clear night they would be there and the sight of them cheered me on.

There was no end to the big freeze, the hospital was full of people with broken bones according to the local paper, then I fell one day while slithering about my goat-keeping chores, shaken, I took to wearing some old woolly socks over my shoes, (I cannot imagine where the idea came from, but I rather think it must have been something that was done in the old days, that had stuck in my mind) they worked well gripping the frozen ground, it certainly wouldn't do to break a leg, it didn't bear thinking about. All trace of sun had gone, the world seemed permanently grey and unbelievably cold. After leaving the children at school, I had to work hard to keep warm, and keep my spirits up; I couldn't remember such a long unrelentingly cold and cheerless winter.

Then one Sunday Ben came running up

the garden path to the kitchen door at tea-time, nearly there, he tripped, and flew straight through the glass, it was one big sheet and simply disintegrated all around him. I was there and could hardly bear to look, I ran across the room, to help him, but with legs like lead it seemed to take forever, he was very calm and we managed to take off his jumper with all the glass bits on it, and threw it straight in the bin, everyone left their various occupations and came running to see what the tremendous bang had been. Miraculously Ben was perfectly alright, not even a tiny scratch on him, but on the floor was a sight to make one blanch, all around lay huge long pointed shards of glass, any one of which could have killed him, I was convinced! These days glass for doors is reinforced in some way to make it safe, but when we moved in I had no idea that our back door was a danger.

The first thing was to gently brush all the tiny specks off Ben and out of his hair, I thought talcum powder would help "unstick" them, followed by a nice hot bath and hoped that every last bit would wash off him and out of his hair. As it was Sunday evening we would have to wait till next day for a glazier, and already the temperature in the kitchen had plummeted, I didn't like the idea of a night with no proper door. John and David decided to swing themselves up into the attic and see what could be found up there, there should be some bits of carpet left over from the sitting-room, or stairs, and thank goodness there were. We had gradually been assembling a few tools for emergencies over the years, so were able to produce a hammer and nails, and between us nailed the carpet pieces over the door frame, then they went down to the garage and found a few odd pieces of wood, which we nailed across on the inside to make it as secure as possible. Delilah and I slept with the bedroom door open that night so that we might hear any intruders! When the glaziers finally came, several days later they assured me that what they were putting in was toughened glass.

John and David had been keeping a close eye on the little pond near Daisy's shed, and one week-end said firmly that it was at last safe to slide across, and all four of them spent the entire weekend sliding skilfully round and round, while I cooked filling and warming meals to keep us going for a bit, and made hot drinks for everyone, whilst keeping a wary eye on the proceedings from the warm kitchen.

They showed off their skating and shared the delight of their very own rink with Mr. and Mrs Phipps when they called in to make sure we were alright in our new home, they joined in the fun and had some hot cups of tea before they left, confessing that they felt reassured now they had seen everything for themselves, and how happily we had fitted into our new life. Richard and Hilary who had started us off with our goat-keeping had also been out to see us, on the day we had inadvertently locked ourselves out of the house and the key refused to work again. Luckily for us we bumped into them in the little town, and when Kate told them what had happened they insisted on coming home with us, and Richard found the knack of it, and assured himself that we could work it before they left, after giving it a drop of oil to be on the safe side. A few days later coming home from school we were astounded to find a large pile of logs outside the front door, and a note pushed through the letter-box from Hilary, "Sorry to have missed you, Richard has been cutting up some old branches, and we thought you could use them on your fire, - the half sack of locust beans are for Daisy - just a handful or so each day." We were quite over-whelmed and delighted to have a wonderful crackling fire each evening when we got home, and Daisy crunched up her treat with enthusiasm.

Finally to my great relief the freezing

weather came to an end, though February began in torrential downpours, and whenever I raced down the garden to care for Daisy, at least three times a day, I noticed a very unpleasant miasma permeating the garden, I could have sworn it was drains, very bad ones, but I knew they were alright had I not been told that the council took care of the septic tank, and one need never give it a thought? I peered uncertainly at the kitchen drain, it was definitely not draining, and indeed it was beginning to overflow into the garden. Horrified I rang the Council and was informed that it was not due to be done for another six months, but when I described the problem and told them I had a family of young children they did turn up, and pumped it all out. We had a problem with this septic tank for years, with me ringing them practically monthly to deal with it, until one day someone in another part of the country went to court about the very same problem, and the Judge was amazed that such things still existed (that was a communal one, as ours had turned out to be), he thought it must be the last one in the country, and I believe recommended that it should be done away with, and mains drainage installed, our council must have read the same paper, as after about ten years of problems with it, we too were allowed mains drainage, and heaved a huge sigh of relief.

Well, as my mother put it there are always "teething problems" with a new property, and now Daisy found one, clearly bored as the weather had kept her indoors so much, she set about modifying her lovely goat-shed, and to my horror easily knocked a huge hole in the wall! This was catastrophic! I knew it wouldn't be long before she just walked out, the thought of her leaping over all the walls, and eating the contents of everyone's gardens one by one made me cold with foreboding. There was nothing for it but to tether her both inside as well as out for the time being. However, I had a very good goat-book which told one everything one needed to know about goats and their care, and also incredibly, how to make a goat-house from those rough outside pieces of tree-trunk, cut in long pieces when planks were made. So it was that we discovered our local family owned sawmill and sure enough we were able to pick up these amazing bits very cheaply, and much nicer than planks with the bark still attractively attached. Each day after leaving everyone at school, I loaded a few more pieces into the mini and ferried them carefully back to join the hay, straw, oats, furniture and garden tools in the garage. I discovered sadly though that none of us seemed capable of renovating Daisy's house, the boys were just too young, and although I wanted to, it just defeated me.

As problems never come singly, it was also necessary to find a blacksmith, if one has a goat to tether one needs an iron bar shaped like a corkscrew, with a revolving piece at the top, this fits to a swivel on the end of your goat chain and will go round and round for ever without the goat tying itself in knots, and also without her pulling her stake out of the ground, which she was wont to do whenever she got bored, or caught sight of a plant I hoped to preserve. Luckily I remembered that with the goat society there is always good advice at the end of the phone, and so there was, and we had the pleasure of finding that blacksmiths were still about, and when we found the smithy there were the sparks from the fire flying up, just like the old days.

How lucky that there was a horse being shod when we arrived, the children were thrilled while we waited quietly and watched the blacksmith remove the last one of its shoes, as it stood there calmly in the midst of what seems to me a primevally noisy and dramatic setting. He filed its hooves, selected the shoes, and tried each one for size against the horse's feet, then put each one into the fire till it glowed red hot and white hot, we could feel the heat on our faces as it was carried over to the anvil, and moved this way and that and hammered into the right shape to be a perfect fit and the ancient scent of a working smithy, a mixture of horn and hot coals, assailed our nostrils as he plunged each shoe into water where it dramatically hissed and steamed while it cooled, and the patient horse stood still while each foot was lifted up in turn, and the cooled shoe, which nevertheless hissed and steamed alarmingly, was fitted and then hammered onto the hoof with those special square nails which the blacksmith removed one by one from his mouth.

"Oh poor horse!" exclaimed Kate, "It's alright," explained John, who had read about it, "It doesn't hurt the horse, his hooves are giant toenails." "It's got to be done carefully though, by someone who knows what he is doing." I added, not wanting to run the risk of anyone experimenting! I was so glad that they had seen this happening. I had seen it so often at the smithy in our village when I was a child, and now where are they? Then it was our turn and we explained our need and watched the blacksmith choose a length of iron, which he heated up as he had the horse-shoes, and then begin to hammer it and shape it cleverly on his anvil, heating it again and again until it became a long screw rather like a giant corkscrew which we could screw into the ground, so that now Daisy could be moved from one part of the garden to another, and kept away from any precious plants! Though there were times when; looking as if butter wouldn't melt in her mouth, and studiously ignoring some just beginning to thrive little bush; as soon as she felt me disengage her tether, she would rocket over to it and grab great mouthfuls before she could be stopped! These are things one must put up with if keeping goats in unsuitable surroundings!!!

When we got home the telephone was ringing and the children fell over themselves in their hurry to get in and answer it, "Its Granny", said John, coming back out again, "Someone she knows is coming over to look at the goat-house, this afternoon, and he is a goat-keeper too!" This was wonderful, he surveyed the problem and knew exactly what to do and almost completely rebuilt the shed, using the pieces of wood with the bark still on nailed to the existing frame work and keeping the roof of course, then another lot running a different way, had to be nailed to the inside, with something between to keep out any wind and rain. I believe it was he who also divided it into stalls as it was far too big, and this was just what was needed, as time would tell! The goat house had indeed been a big worry, so the relief was huge, knowing Daisy was at last safe and properly housed, in a shed which would accommodate her and her progeny in spacious comfort.

In my early life I had never under any circumstances asked anyone for help, somehow I always felt one should stand on one's own feet, and not be a burden to anyone else. Now I found that without asking, nevertheless kindnesses and really tremendous help seemed to come our way when we were in need. So often one was at a loss to repay, beyond heartfelt and grateful thanks. Often when one cannot repay a kindness, one finds the odd occasion when someone else has a need that is within one's ability to fulfil so in a way it gets passed on from person to person. When it was a question of payment I was always charged the minimum I felt, and not exploited.

When we had time to examine what we had in the garden properly, it was most exciting. There was lots of Rhubarb, which although not our favourite thing, could be sold; there were currant bushes, and several apple trees, one of which turned out to be a Victoria plum instead! What a wonderful surprise that was when we discovered it one day, later in the year covered with lots of delicious purple plums. There was also plenty of room for growing vegetables to our hearts content. The soil was different here, not stony and grey as in our previous garden, but red, and heavy and very sticky where it had not been cultivated recently. It was still too wet to touch, so we turned our thoughts to livestock. It seemed a pity to waste our pond so we thought ducks might be rather fun, the eggs could be used in cooking. There was a small hut alongside the garage which would do to keep them in, as we were keeping the lovely little hen house, which naturally we had brought with us, for our next batch of hens. However the ducks were a disappointment, they did not grow into nice fat white little things as I had expected, but were tall and rangy, and utterly refused to swim happily about on the pond as we had hoped they would. In due time they were to be despatched for the freezer, but the night before I had such terrible nightmares that it was my "ex" being got rid of in this way, that I resolved never to keep ducks again!

Time kept rushing by and before I had time to think about it Daisy had successfully produced twins. As the weather became more and more spring-like Kate had taken to visiting the goat-house before breakfast, just to see, and this morning came running back in huge excitement to announce the News! We were all electrified, although expected, we could hardly believe it when we rushed down the garden and peered round the door into the largest stall, (quietly, not to disturb the little family,) to see not only Daisy as usual but two very tiny snow white baby kids lying beside her, she seemed pleased to see us, and was as gentle and loving towards us as to her very much alive new family! We quietly attended to her needs, and when the little kids began to search for milk, Kate and I helped them to locate it, this always seemed to be necessary at the beginning, each time she kidded, as Daisy was rather an odd shape, but once they got the hang of it, all was well.

Once we had discovered that Daisy had cleverly produced a boy and a girl, we had to think up names for them. I hastily decided there and then to call all the male goats henceforth "Fred", we didn't want to get too attached to them as they would not stay with us for very long, we had no need, or facilities, for male goats. We intended to breed up, and if our fortunes improved to have a small herd and be commercial about it all (I had constantly hoped to eventually have a proper small-holding and produce goats milk and cheese) I suggested that it would be a good idea to have a theme for our goats names, and suggested Herbs, so the little girl kid became "Parsley". For the time being we had to keep Daisy and her kids, loose in her shed at night and during bad weather, and tethered in the garden during the day, the kids ran free of course, but stayed near their mother and all was well. We let the lawn grow to become a paddock and in due course it became necessary to fence it, as I certainly didn't want to keep Daisy permanently tethered.

Life now took on a new momentum, the children had a full social life and most weekends were taken up ferrying them to various friends, or happenings at the school, or indeed having friends to lunch and generally tea as well. Luckily they enjoyed the goats and exploring the woods, and, as we were only a short distance from another beach, we went there for walks, rock-pooling, or just kicking a ball all over the sand. Delilah loved the firm sand beneath her paws, and chased the boys and the ball enthusiastically to everyone's delight, she looked so funny chasing this ball which was larger than her, pushing it along with her nose and of course, quite unable to pick it up however hard she tried, she barked at it excitedly, tail wagging non-stop as she joined in the game. She was such an important part of the family, and went everywhere with us, though sometimes if the weather was too hot for her in the summer, or we were going to a school play or something where she absolutely had to stay behind, she would always settle in her basket and doze until we got back.

An odd thing was that all through those cold winter nights during the first early weeks, as I walked down through the garden to tend to the goats after the children were in bed, I could see all the little lighted windows in neighbouring houses, which gave a friendly impression, but who lived in them, what were they like? There was never a sign of life however, not in the mornings when we left for school, nor in the evenings when we returned. It seemed very odd and in time the lights seemed less friendly, unreal, where were the inhabitants, would they ever appear and why was one of the houses never lit up? It seemed lonely and sad, and rather eerie. I tried to put them out of my mind, and succeeded so well over the whole of the winter period, that it was an enormous surprise, when one sunny spring day as I backed the car out of the garage a beaming figure with one gold and one black tooth, suddenly appeared, "like a gnome out of the ground", I thought a little wildly. I got out to close the garage door. "Good morning!" he said. I tried to pull myself together; the situation seemed so unreal at first. I smiled back. "I am one of your neighbours," he went on, "I don't expect you have met any yet, have you?" I shook my head, "Well," he said pointing to each house in turn, and by way of introduction, proceeding to recite the names of the occupants of each. "You'll see them soon enough now the weather's improving." A thought struck him, "All except that one, (pointing to the empty house) he is in hospital. Not expected to come out." he added gloomily. "Oh, I am sorry," I said, and, as he turned away, "Thank-you for introducing every-one!" I sent up a prayer for the lonely little house's owner, started up the car again, and we set off for school.

Chapter 11
Neighbours

There were no further signs of our neighbours for the time being, but the eerie feeling had been dispelled, and we had a lot to do, first I collected up some of the overflow of possessions stored in the garage and sold them off, advertising items of furniture in the local paper, and this and that to junk shops, and once that was done I got on the telephone and ordered some more hens, we definitely needed our lovely new laid eggs back, then the next weekend we made a concerted effort to fence off the vegetable patch before our new hens arrived, once we had all our vegetables in the ground we didn't want to the hens to even notice them if possible! We managed to do this because first John, then David found bits of fence panelling amongst the undergrowth in the garden when first exploring, then Ben and Kate started to see what they could find and eventually they discovered bits of wood and wire all over the place like buried treasure! The binder twine that arrived in abundance on every bale of hay and straw was useful for tying bits of odd shaped wood together, so on the whole though not a thing of beauty, but it did work reasonably well as long as we whisked the goats quickly past. Over the years we were forever concocting fences in different parts of the garden to keep things out or in, with varying degrees of success at first!

The hens arrived in due course, and after the usual hesitant start that poor battery hens exhibit, decided this must be heaven, and were soon clucking contentedly about the garden, quite unfazed by children and goats dashing up and down, it was lovely to have hens back in our lives again, and they soon began producing lovely brown eggs for our breakfast, and we could have more homemade cakes. It was very cheering when our nearest neighbours popped a head over the fence and asked if we would sell them half a dozen of our newly laid eggs, and made this a regular arrangement. I suddenly realised one day, that after feeling like a fish out of water in the beginning, finally and imperceptibly we had all put down our roots, the tiny house had magically seemed to expand to accommodate us, it no longer felt as if we were living in a caravan, and Daisy was no longer dependent on us being her herd, now that she had started one of her own and had their company it made things much easier.

One day my contented frame of mind received a jolt, the children were all at school one morning when arriving home with the groceries, and carrying armfuls of flour, sugar and various other necessities through to the kitchen; I inadvertently dropped my key-ring with all our keys onto the work-surface too, before taking a bag of oats down to the bin in the garage where they were stored, and on my return found the front door had slammed shut! The utter finality of it sank in as I hopefully examined all the windows and doors, there must be one surely, that I could prise open and climb in, but they were all out of reach and perversely they were all very firmly closed! I went back to the garage looking for something to stand on, there was a shabby old chair I used as a saw horse, so carried that back up the garden, and stood on it trying to reach a small window in the dining-room, the latch was loose and jiggled a bit, but not enough. Oh Horrors, now what was I to do! Beginning to feel a bit desperate, and looking round for inspiration I beheld across next door's garden, in the lane, the one neighbour we'd met already with another larger, broader man, they were both standing there and staring, mumchance, as though rooted unhelpfully to the spot. I felt distinctly foolish and rather nettled, shouldn't they be offering to help, I thought crossly? How long had they been standing there watching my discomfiture?

I advanced towards the low wall, dividing my garden from the next. "I'm locked out," I called "What on earth am I going to do?" Men were generally good at such problems I believed. For a moment I didn't think they were going to reply. The smaller of the two made as if to turn and make his escape, but the taller one called back, "You'll have to break a window!" I was startled "Break it?" I quavered. "It's all you can do." Perhaps I looked as horrified as I felt. "Never mind, I'll come over after dinner, and put another pane in for you!" and with that he too turned and stumped away, towards the house which had always had no light in its windows!

Well that was very kind, and things didn't look quite so bleak, but break a window! Easier said than done, there is a built-in taboo it seems to me that has to be over-come first, and what does one break it with, I wondered looking around for the perfect tool. Standing on my chair, and feeling guiltily like a vandal I tapped gently on the tiny quarter light with a small stone. That didn't work so back to the garage I went and finally found a hammer! That should do the trick! Standing on my chair I hammered in one corner of the small window with progressively harder blows, until it finally shattered, and reaching down through the hole I was able to open the larger window and climb in! By the time the shopping was stored away, the broken glass swept up, and pangs of hunger assuaged, my new neighbour was back, miraculously with a piece of glass which he then cut to size in the kitchen, and fitted in place with some putty and no fuss. He would accept no payment, saying he had lots of glass left over from his greenhouse, but he accepted a cup of tea, and sat on the kitchen stool while I prepared supper for when the children came home, he told me his name was John Goode, that he had indeed been in hospital and had not expected to come out, but, here he was after all. He told me how he and his wife had brought up a family in that house, but he was on his own now, he had a kind daughter who cooked and brought things round for him, but he could cook himself and made a very good pasty on occasion!

That weekend I made a chocolate cake and asked John and David to take it over, with our thanks for mending the window. "Don't stay long as he has only just come out of hospital, and may be very tired!" they came running excitedly back in due course "He said thank your mother very much for the cake!" John began, as David interrupted "He was very nice, he asked what we did with ourselves, and we told him we go fishing sometimes!" "And he told us," John went on joyfully, "That eels go up our leat and told us how to catch them!" "You have to go down when it gets dark with a torch!" said David, his eyes shining. "Not at this time of year though." "That's amazing, right past our garden!" I exclaimed, enjoying their enthusiasm. After all perhaps they would forget before it actually came to catching one themselves, I thought hopefully. After that I often saw him about, once leaning over the wall talking to Daisy, he had made friends with her apparently by offering her a banana, and was never tired of bringing one over for her, it amused him the way she manoeuvred it around finally eating it, skin and all. I concealed my horror, as no harm had been done, but one has to be careful, some things are lethal to goats! I never told him, as by now I knew he had cancer, and was so glad that he found pleasure looking at the animals, and coming over from time to time.

He saw me planting out runner beans rather hurriedly one morning; standing in the gateway he surveyed the scene, I was rather pleased with all my healthy little plants, and this was the second sowing this year. "Makes me sea-sick!" he announced. Had I heard aright? Was he ill? I rushed and fetched the old chair from the garage, "What's that for?" he enquired. "You! You'd better sit down for a minute!" He chuckled - "No, I'm alright, it's just your wavy rows, makes me sea-sick, looking at them!" He took my trowel, "You leave them to me, you'll have plenty to do, I'll be bound!" I took the hint and left him to it, as he fetched his own spade, and began to tidy up my two rows. I did the usual quick tidying chores, and put the washing into the machine, and began to peel the potatoes for supper that evening. When I saw from the kitchen window that he had finished, I went down to look. He had put up canes for each bean plant as well, and it looked like a proper vegetable garden, I was delighted, as my earlier row leaned rather drunkenly to one side! Then he came to see what was in the greenhouse, the tomatoes plants were big and bushy, healthy and lush, but there was something indefinably wrong somewhere, I couldn't think what. "You need to pinch those out!" he opined. "What?" said I, and "How?" So he showed me how to remove the excess branches which appeared between the stem and leaf all the way up, some had grown quite large already, "You'll get larger tomatoes now." Now I knew why all the tomatoes at the old house had been numerous enough, but really quite small. "Then you tie them in to a cane each, like this." He added. I showed him my green peppers at the end of the green house, and the cucumber, but he didn't evince much interest in them. "I must be off, visiting my daughter this afternoon!" and away he went.

When I collected the children I told them how Mr. Goode had been so kind and what he had done for us, and wondered what we could do for him in return. Eventually we decided to ask him if he would like to come to supper with us one evening, to save him cooking for himself for once, and began to wonder worriedly what on earth to make, however it was soon decided that it should be Fish pie, a recipe originally concocted by my mother, which was everyone's favourite. This was a good idea as it could be made the day before, so too could an Orange Flan, which was my concoction, so with my supportive team to help entertain I felt a bit more confident, to ask him when he next appeared. This was not for some time however.

Then one week-end Kate announced in

her bright clear voice, "Mum, there's a miner in the garden!" A miner, what did she know about miners, I wondered looking out of the window, to see a large black clad back, with a large black hat on its head, walking quickly away down the path, and on the back door step was the biggest most succulent lettuce I'd ever seen. "Kate that is Mr. Goode, could you catch him, and ask if he would like to have supper with us, about seven thirty next Friday?" Only the boys had met him so far, but she had been most impressed by his kindness to us, and immediately ran down the path before he vanished, the large figure paused and looked down at the small neat girl in her blue jeans and red jersey, her cheerful little face turned up to him, he bent down a little to hear what she was saying, and I saw him nodding his head as he gave her his answer, then she turned back to the house, giving him a happy little wave of her hand as she came.

All my life I have been crippled by shyness, possibly because I had very few outside influences in my life until I was ten years old, and at school had no idea how to cope with other children. Being determined to do all that I could, to help my own children, like and be liked by those that came our way. I always told them how kind people were, and indeed they were over all those years, and told them that as we were so poor there was not much we could do in return, but that we would do what we could, and even if we only thanked those who helped us, that at least meant something, and that if they just told people about what they had been doing, their adventures and so on, that would cheer them up and give them pleasure as often they were alone, and without their families. To my delight they were always welcoming and interested in people, and did quite naturally talk away, and people seemed to like that, and were very nice and kind to them.

Friday evening was sunny, warm and lovely. The housework usually had to take second place to livestock and garden, so I hoovered and dusted, and as we had no excess furniture, just the necessities, it didn't take very long to make it look bright and welcoming. John brought an extra chair down from upstairs and I laid the table, with some flowers from the garden in the centre. At this stage all four did something to help when visitors were coming, which was lovely, and seemed to add to the general excitement of a special occasion. When Mr. Goode arrived and came into the room, he seemed taller and broader than ever, and I wondered how he would ever fit, as the whole room and its contents seemed smaller than ever in his presence. Everyone wanted him to sit next to them, so in the end he sat between Kate and Ben and looked across the table at the other two. Everything seemed to go swimmingly, as I brought in the food and served it out and David and Ben passed round the vegetables, and John poured everyone home-made lemonade. Mr. Goode told them how when he had been younger and all the little houses had been filled with children, he would gather them all up and take them over to the field opposite to play cricket, to give their mothers a rest!

He told us how when he was a lad he had worked for the farmer, hay-making, and had been sent to fetch the gallon of cider the men needed to refresh themselves, but on the way back had decided to taste it! He warned us that cider is different from other alcohol, as you can feel perfectly fine whilst drinking it, but when you wish to stand up - you are legless!!! It was due to this fact the local cider bar would never sell more than one glass to any woman, and only two to any man!

When Kate got a bit sleepy, I took her up to bed, and settled her down, before we had coffee. Apparently in the old days, before the man who'd owned our house had bought up all the little bits of land which people could no longer cope with as they got older, a large part of our garden had belonged to Mr. Goode, and he and his son had grown all the vegetables the family needed on it! So we were following tradition, which was heartening to hear. At times, he told us the river rose, and covered the garden and the lane, running into the cellars of those who had them, but we were not to worry about this, our house was on higher ground and the water never reached it. When in fact this happened some years later, we remembered his words and were reassured, and the water soon receded and no harm was done.

In his later years he had become a bell-ringer at the church across the fields. David said that he enjoyed playing the guitar, and Mr. Goode thought they would probably all enjoy bell-ringing as they got a bit older, they would always be welcome, he told them. By the time he went home that evening, we felt that we had learnt a lot of useful local knowledge, and his wisdom and kindness were to touch our lives for the rest of that year.

On days when one did not see him at all there would often be a lovely lettuce reposing on the mat when we got back from school. When we thanked him, he told us that he had a friend who ran a market garden, who'd grown so many lettuces he couldn't give them away! Occasionally too there would be a cardboard box of greens, not good enough to sell, for Daisy, outside our backdoor. How to repay? He would not come to supper again, but accepted a cup of tea, now and then "if I was having one", so I who never stopped for cups of tea, suddenly developed a need for one now and again, if I encountered him in the lane, or looking over the wall talking to Daisy. We would settle down as if we had all the time in the world, and talk over everything that occurred to us, as comfortably as if we had known each other all our lives.

I was concerned about what he had to face, but he told me he had great faith. He reckoned he had been a sinner in his youth, though that was never explained. When he lost his wife he didn't know what to do, but the same neighbour who had so suddenly appeared one day outside my garage, had, invited him to accompany them to church one day. Mr. Goode had turned him down, "They'll think I'm sissy, I'm not going off to church on a Sunday morning, for everyone to see!"

However, the kind neighbour had persevered, "Come with me to Evensong, then!

No-one you know goes then." So he had, and after that he had often gone up to the Vicarage for a chat with the old Vicar, he reckoned that the old man was lonely, rattling around all by himself in that big cold old house. They too had found they could talk away an evening, the Vicar had opened his eyes to so much that had brought him great comfort, and he reckoned that they cheered each other up. The Vicar had teased him about his prowess with a pasty - I'll make you one, then you'll see, said Mr. Goode, and so he had - leaving it in his porch for him to find after Evensong one evening. He was delighted and amused that the next time he went to Church the Vicar had come flying down the church, brandishing the dish on high, through all the congregation, crying out that it was the best pasty he'd ever tasted! "Through all the congregation! Laughing away, he didn't care! He is a one, that Vicar!"

So the last little house across the lane, had its windows cheerfully lit at night like the others, and I knew as I went up and down with Daisy, who still had to be milked in the kitchen while she ate her oats, and then back and fore with her clean water for the night, and her bundle of hay, that the stalwart soul within was holding his own, in his terrible battle, and

I offered up my prayers for the well-being of this brave and kindly man.

Throughout the rest of the year he was always about, his windows lit up at night, and his back door open during the day as mine always was in the warmer weather, I hated to shut the summer out, and loved the scents of the flowers and trees wafting into the house. I always wanted to blur the edges between out and in, and picked flowers and foliage for indoors which helped when the door had to be closed.

He noticed this and told me that his wife had been the same, but warned me never to go upstairs leaving the door open, "always lock your doors" he told me, I was surprised at this, and told him that I never did, but he was shocked, and said we were too near the town and one never knew who might be about! So I was more careful after that.

One day, Ben, who had been given money for his birthday by various relatives, decided that he wanted a football, so off we went to our favourite sports-shop, which saw a lot of my family over the years! It was the perfect place to whet ones appetite; even I enjoyed looking at all the equipment, for every sporting activity under the sun! As we wandered round, looking at this Aladdin's cave, I rather hoped that Ben might plump for another less potentially hazardous present. - Some hopes! We consulted with a helpful man who knew all about his merchandise, and went home eventually, after much careful thought, and comparison, one with another, with the best ball that his money could buy. This was great, they all had a wonderful time each evening kicking it about on our lovely large lawn, and it was even better when friends came and joined in at the weekends. Unfortunately, as was inevitable, because it takes time and practice to make perfect, the poor old greenhouse suffered a direct hit one evening. We were all horrified, but it was getting late and time for bed, so after making sure that there was no glass left out on the path to cut any little animals' feet, we went indoors leaving the problem for tomorrow.

By the time I got around to the broken pane next morning it was past mid-day, I swept up the last of the glass inside the green-house, and then looked for the hole in the roof, but there wasn't one, not in the side, nor anywhere. As I came out, there was Mr. Goode chuckling at my mystification, "I heard it go," he said, "So as I have a few panes left from my old greenhouse I came over and fixed it after you all went off this morning!" He brushed aside my thanks, "There'll be a few more, I reckon, before they get the hang of it, but don't you worry, I've still got some left, and some putty!" So the panes were mended, and the skill with the ball improved.

Occasionally there was a visit to the hospital, but reassuringly Mr. Goode would reappear to feed Daisy a banana or have a cup of tea, and we would talk of everything under the sun, until the day finally came when a kind neighbour came around to tell me that he had gone to hospital when I'd been out, and had asked them to let me know. The last time I saw him was in that hospital bed, a sweet young nurse told me where to find him, and I took comfort from the fact that he had someone so gentle to care for him, and that he would soon be with his dear wife, and his suffering over.

Chapter 12
Mary Plain

One morning having dropped everyone off at school, I made one of my periodic visits to a nearby farm which we had discovered shortly after our move, where the farmer kindly sold me hay and straw when I needed them for the goats. Today he looked worried as I backed the mini up to the huge open barn. I followed him in and found the huge space where bales were normally stacked, had been rearranged and divided up with hurdles forming small rooms in each of which was a pregnant sheep, or one whose lambs had already had been born. There was an air of calm "business" about the place, mother sheep made loving little grunts to their offspring, and Mr. Toms walked quietly amongst them talking encouragingly to them, they looked at him trustfully, none of them showed any sign of nervousness, they were as content to let him be near them as any household pet might be. The roof of the building was very high and the walls stopped some way below it, so the whole place was airy and cool, but the sheep were protected from the worst of the weather and had their lambs successfully, keeping them sheltered for the first few weeks of their lives.

However this morning, calm, imperturbable Mr. Toms was looking worried. "I wonder if you could help me?" He asked. One of the ewes was having difficulty, and Mr. Toms' daughter who usually helped on these occasions was away in the town that morning. He turned to me, his hands were too big for the job he said, and he wondered if I could check out what the trouble was? I certainly wanted to help, but was I up to it I wondered, squeamishly. I had not even been present at any of Daisy's kiddings, though once I saw a bitch whelp, and rubbed her puppies with a towel to help her with a large litter. I couldn't leave Mr. Toms or the poor sheep in the lurch, so trying to keep a calm exterior I shakily rolled up my sleeves, and washed in the bucket of soapy water he had there feeling a bit like a vet in one of those TV programmes. Hoping I could do it and talking soothingly to the sheep I gently pushed my hand inside her till I could feel something, Mr. Toms was giving me directions, and I was doing my best to make sense of what I could feel. At this point a bicycle rolled in bearing nothing less than what seemed to be the village bobby! For one crazy moment I thought salvation had come, but one glance showed that his hands were not one whit smaller than the farmers.

Oh Lord it was all down to me, here were two burly men highly competent in their own field paying me the huge compliment of thinking I could rise to the occasion. Desperately I tried again, it seemed that one foreleg was forward, and one back, Mr. Toms told me I should hook the other one forwards too - easier said than done, but there was no giving up, it had to be done, the sheep and I were in this together, and the ordeal seemed to go on far too long, but at long last - somehow it came right, the sheep seemed to sense it at once, and to my utter joy I was able to draw the little lamb out, Mr. Toms took over at once and swung the little creature back and fore to get air into its lungs. It breathed, and he gave it to its mother to suckle and get the all-important colostrum it needed for health. I washed my hands and arms feeling utterly euphoric, when I looked at the Policeman and Mr. Toms I realised delightedly that both of them felt very much the same way. The Policeman kept saying that was a very good job, and with a big smile all round announced he'd better be off, and mounting his bike cycled slowly back down the lane. I felt a million dollars, and when the hay I needed was loaded up, the little mini flew home way above the hedgerows so light-hearted was my mood!

The next time I went down to the farm it was to collect some bales of straw, and as Mr. Toms loaded some up for me, "I have a lamb here you could have to rear yourself!" He said as if it was the most ordinary thing in the world, "One of them had triplets and I don't want to be bothered, bottle-feeding it." And that's when I heard my own voice thanking him very much! I was shocked, but before I could say another word, he had brought over, not the sort of lamb one normally thinks of, white and reasonably big enough to cuddle, but a very small putty-coloured thing that resembled nothing so much as a piece of string, which he put into my arms! I stared at it while Mr. Toms made a nest for it in a box amongst the bales, then I looked at him as the awful thought occurred to me "But I must be mad, I don't know anything about sheep!" He remained utterly calm, "You'll have to give it a bottle for a bit, I can let you have one of those and a teat." He went to the back of the barn, and returned with what looked like a lemonade bottle with a teat on the end, He told me I would have to get some special milk powder from the Farmers Association, and some lamb pellets for when it grew big enough to have them. "Don't over feed it mind!" He said as he explained exactly how to make up the milk "It will all be written down on the packet anyway." I didn't seem to be able to get out of this, one moment of madness, is what it was. I had been teaching myself recently to say "YES PLEASE!" to kind offers, instead of "Oh no! Really I couldn't possibly." Then seeing something really useful, being put away in a drawer or sent to a jumble sale because I was too shy to admit the need and accept. Now look where it had got me! "Don't worry if it dies, I shan't!" He threw in for good measure. So that is how Mary Plain joined the family.

I collected the milk as instructed, and popped the sleeping lamb, into the airing cupboard, unloaded the car, did the chores and thought about how we were to manage. Later, working in the kitchen a slightly aggravating high-pitched noise relentlessly filled the air, one of our neighbours with an electric drill, obviously, but when I looked, all was quiet outside the back-door, whilst inside the house the noise continued. "Help, it must be the lamb" I thought, dashing upstairs and peering round the airing cupboard door, where a wobbly head waved about over the edge of the box, demanding immediate attention. It looked so pathetic maternal instinct took over, suddenly it all seemed quite easy, I left it there and marched downstairs to make up its milk, good heavens, there was nothing to it! I would feed it every four hours like a baby, and all would be well!

The family were electrified when I collected them later that day and told them what was waiting in the airing cupboard and Kate couldn't wait to give Mary Plain her bottle. She was a miracle lamb, thin and puny, unprepossessing, but lion-hearted and totally happy with our arrangements, never faltering in her determination to enjoy her bottle and grow stronger by the day and eventually becoming a good-looking and extremely intelligent member of the family! She soon progressed to a bed in the kitchen, corralled under a shelf with a bed of straw out of any draughts, but she seemed restless and when I decided to cut out the 2 AM feed we moved her down to the goat house behind her own partition with lots of nice warm straw, where it became clear she thought of herself as one of the goats. Sheep, of course being flock animals, need to be with the others; luckily the goats fulfilled this need for her.

As she grew bigger she loved having the

children around at the weekends, and when they and some friends were playing rounders, Mary Plain dashed delightedly around after them, with her tail going round and round in circles too, in the most impossible manner. She and Delilah joined in any chasing games, running after the children or each other with great pleasure. Once when Kate was ill in bed, Mary pushed open the back door, ran up the stairs and sprang upon the bed to keep her company! Not a good idea really, as she would get far too hot indoors with her woolly coat on, but cheering for Kate nevertheless. We were all amazed by her intelligence, and concluded that it was due to being treated like a member of the family, and talked to, she must have listened as she would come to whichever one of us called her name.

We always learnt all we could before we started any venture, but that was never the end of it, we all of us never stopped learning as we went along. Daisy soon made it plain that it was high time we removed the kids. Kate was shocked, "Daisy is being horrid to her babies, butting them if they go near her!" I brought her up the garden where I could keep an eye on her through the kitchen window, John cleaned out her water bucket and filled it afresh and put it where she could reach it at the end of her tether, no nearer or it would be upset. Sure enough she would not let them suckle, and they had to stay a judicious distance away from her. After that we put them in with Mary, and let Daisy enjoy her well-earned peace.

In the early part of the year the goats and Mary went into the enclosure we had made round the "lawn", then when they were older and much larger I was able to take all of them up the footpath to browse on the large area of rough pasture which appeared to belong to nobody, and adjoined the stream and the trees beyond our garden. Each day on a fresh area of pasture, and not too close to the trees, goats are browsers, and having read of one that hanged itself by getting its chain over a branch which it had pulled down, which had then sprung up with fatal consequences, I was always extremely careful. At first we took it in turns to stay for a while and keep Mary company, and then bring her home. However one weekend when we'd all been there enjoying the sun, and having a picnic, the children had run home ahead of me and Mary, determined to catch them, was leading the way back. Suddenly my worst fears were realised when a big black rangy dog, without any humans in tow appeared, it looked fierce to me and growled, I was glad that Delilah and the children were safely home, I could hear them in the garden, it looked at me and then at Mary, and clearly thinking this was a lamb to the slaughter, quickened his pace eyeing Mary and expecting her to run away, but she was quite obviously delighted to see him, someone else to play with!!! She trotted towards the dog enthusiastically, her tail going round and round, and the dog stopped in sheer disbelief, Mary was disappointed at this and began to bounce up and down with all four feet together to encourage him, the dog shrank back in total horror, whirled round and ran back the way he had come as fast as he could with his tail between his legs, Mary in hot pursuit, with me bringing up the rear, hanging on to her lead and trying to slow her down, without much success, until we reached our own gate, desperately I dug in my heels, and pulled her towards it, and hearing the children she turned in and trotted down the garden path as good as gold, I didn't worry about her after that!

As the weather got warmer, after leaving the children at school, I would dash home, milk Daisy and take all the animals up the footpath. This meant walking up with one or two and carefully tethering them, and running back as fast as possible for the next two; the whole proceedings in reverse by the afternoon. Mary, being an independent sort of sheep, had her own arrangement, she could be tied to a large cow-parsley or similar weed near enough to the goats for company and there she stayed as long as she felt like it, and then surprised me by appearing outside the kitchen door when she had eaten her fill! This became her normal routine, and I would take her down to the Lawn/paddock and shut her in.

I kept weekends as free as goat-keeping allows, for the children and gardened during the week. There was already plenty of rhubarb to be picked, and I was able to sell that, and in due course the currant bushes produced a wonderful crop, I made some red-currant jelly, and sold the rest. I grew Money-maker tomatoes in the big greenhouse as they sounded like a good omen, and grown in the lovely compost we made from weed tops, and the stuff that came out of Daisy's shed all rotted down, they tasted absolutely delicious, (though the first year we used the manure from our friends stables, we didn't have so far to go to collect it now!)

Despite hearing that they needed different conditions, I also successfully grew lovely succulent sweet peppers and cucumbers in my greenhouse, and sold some of them, specially the tomatoes of which there were masses. Next I sowed broad and runner-beans, in boxes and old plastic bowls in there as well! I was waiting for the clay soil to dry out and trying to get a head start as well. Finally the day came, however, and I planted out a lovely double row of runner beans, each with two new little leaves unfurling at the top, but when I came down the garden the following morning, there to my utter disbelief were two rows of topless green stems!! However, I had started early, and there was time to begin again, this time I only planted them out when the leaves were large, and there were two more appearing on top, this time the slugs and snails left them alone.

When they were approaching the top of their canes I sowed another double row, and that had been when Mr. Goode appeared on the scene and showed me how to do it properly! The broad beans were dwarf ones, and picked when the beans inside the pods are no bigger than ones thumbnail were not in the least like those large floury tough skinned ones that all too often appeared on ones plate in the past, and again I put in a second crop, to prolong the season; French beans too as David said he liked them, and of course carrots, beetroot, and turnips. I hoped to keep us supplied all year, and to get a freezer and freeze them eventually, also the milk while it was plentiful, to keep us going when it waned during the winter months.

Every afternoon I would bring the goats home and put all the animals safely in their big shed. They soon got used to the routine and flopped down contentedly to chew the cud. The partitions were too high for them to jump out, but open so that when I left I could leave the main door open to the fresh air. They had an idyllic spot, the stream gurgled past the end of the garden there, and they had the shade of the woods, and apple trees round about them. Together we had manoeuvred the hen house until it reposed under its own little tree on the opposite side of the garden to the stream, but near the goat house, and one could look out of the kitchen window from the top of the garden and see that all was well beyond the pond.

I had been searching our new surroundings for places where I could collect green-stuff for them to eat when they came in. They had their oats in the morning before they went out, and oats and hay in the evenings, but as in an ideal situation they would have been in their own fields all day, (with available shelter against too much sun or rain), it seemed right to bring greenery in for them. Before she kidded Daisy always came with me and between us we browsed the banks and any roadside areas of grass, young nettles and hogs-weed, she eating her fill, and me filling the mini. Once the kids had arrived Daisy stayed with them, but of course Delilah Dachshund who went everywhere with us still came into the woods with me for company while I collected young brambles and ivy, it was quite time consuming and I was trying to think of a solution while driving home one summer morning. We travelled a winding journey, as I searched the country lanes for suitable greenery, away from cars and pollution.

Suddenly I came across a huge mound of the most succulent fresh green-stuff you could imagine, far more than I could normally manage to collect, already cut and piled neatly, at the side of the lane. Oh no! I couldn't bear it, what on earth would we do if it was all cut and taken away, - such a waste! Very slowly I kept going till round the next bend I came upon a pleasant looking man with a cheerful face, wielding a sickle and neatly trimming the summer growth from the bank, even some of the protruding branches from the hedge were coming down, it was beautifully done and looked like a well-tended garden path. There was something about his manner, he seemed at one with the world around him and radiated contentment. I stopped the car and leapt out to speak to him. He seemed a little surprised but stopped what he was doing and listened calmly, Of course I could have the green-stuff for my goats, - "No don't take that over there, try this pile up here its freshly cut and much cleaner, from higher up!"

He helped load a huge amount into the back of the mini and when he'd finished, "Look, if you like, I'll just be a bit further along tomorrow, and if I know you're coming, I'll save any of the good stuff for you!" This was marvellous, lots of lovely good food for the goats, and so very time-saving for me. What a good man he was, a friend in need if ever there was one. From then on throughout that summer he told me where to find him next day, and always filled the little mini with good food for goats, reminding me on Fridays that with the weekend coming up he wouldn't be there, and telling me where he would be on the Monday. It was a blow at the end of the year when he told me he wouldn't be around in the spring as he had reluctantly accepted voluntary redundancy, as the council were cutting down on their work-force.

Next time I went to the farm, Mr. Toms

asked me if I had room for another lamb, I had been telling him how well Mary was getting on with the goats and children, and asking his advice about weaning her, and he sprang his bombshell; I was taken completely by surprise. "It's alright," he said, "It's just that it is the last one, and I can't be bothered to go on bottle feeding it! So if you would take him off my hands? They can both be weaned now, I'll give you some lamb pellets to be going on with, and then you will have to get some more from the Farmers Association." I was so horrified by all this generosity that I demurred a bit, but he managed to convince me that I should take it, and I felt that I had to give in gracefully, it was so incredibly kind, and maybe it was better for Mary to have one of her own kind to talk to.

I had decided to call Mary after a book I'd been given as a child about a little bear called Mary Plain, and she had been very plain and unprepossessing at the beginning, though grew up to be a beautiful sheep. So it was only fair that the next name should be a family decision. We discussed it on the way home in the mini as we so often did when we were all together driving peacefully along. I could pose a question, and then concentrate on the driving, throwing in the odd idea as it occurred, and they would sort it all out. "Is it a boy or a girl?" asked Ben "A boy one - Gosh! A ram, I suppose." I replied. There was no discussion at all really; - "Let's call him Herbie!" They all said at once. We had been taken to see the film of the lovable little car by kind friends who had wanted to give us all a Christmas treat and they had all chosen that in preference to the pantomime.

So Herbie lived with Mary in her stall, and was a delightful white fluffy lamb just as I had imagined them all, before poor little Mary Plain arrived. However, looks are certainly not everything - he was a long-wool cross, I believe, and though I have no knowledge of other long-wools, dear little Herbie was a trifle dim - a contented little lamb, but vague, a bit slow on the up-take, and he could not seem to remember his name! You could stand at the back door with his lamb pellets ready, and call "Herbie! Herbie!" and he would be half-way up the garden path, looking adorable smelling a flower, in a world of his own. Then he would become gradually aware that a voice was buzzing in his ears, and finally he'd look up at you rather absent-mindedly, and you could actually see the light dawn as he registered that this call was for him, he would give a delighted little skip, and then a bigger one as he corkscrewed right up in the air and wagged his tail, then put his head down and come thundering up delighted with himself at remembering who he was, and there were lamb pellets all ready for such a clever lamb!!

Herbie didn't stay with us forever, when the time was right Mr. Toms took him back and saying he would be sold now, insisted on giving me the money he would fetch. Overwhelmed by the tremendous kindness we encountered in those days, I had learned to accept it for the sake of the children, as I definitely wouldn't take a job until they were much older.

When Fred grew big he became a bit of a bully, his horns were still small but one would not want to be on the wrong end of them, and he loved it when everyone played tag or football on the "lawn", and he would try to join in, which could be painful. The female kid had her horns removed humanely by the vet shortly after birth, but it was not worth paying for Fred to be done as well. He wickedly butted the lambs when he got the chance, so we had to keep them apart and one day he thought it great fun to chase the chickens, they squawked and ran about, and before he could be caught, he butted one right into the pond. John hastily enticed him back into his stall with some cabbage leaves, and David and Ben managed to rescue the bedraggled hen. Kate came running into the kitchen with the news that Mrs. Pankhurst was being brought up to the house, and I went to fetch an old towel. We wrapped it round the bedraggled hen, who was soon making contented little noises as she began to feel warm and dry, we gave her some little titbits as well, and ever after that whenever she was let out in the mornings, she made a beeline for the kitchen in case there was something more interesting than layers mash to be found, this amused our neighbours who were in their garden almost as much as we were during the nice weather.

They were the most perfect neighbours who were interested in all the goings on in our corner of the community, and were never anything other than totally supportive of all we did, (I do not think one could ever manage such a thing in this day and age, without having a proper small-holding with licences and things). One day when I arrived home from taking the children to school, I discovered my neighbour and her two small children standing patiently in their garden, holding Daisy with a bit of rope through her collar, and keeping an eye on the kids, Fred had managed to let them all out of the goat-house, and they'd gone exploring!

This meant it was time for him to go. All that we had been learning about self-sufficiency taught me not to be sentimental, but it was a difficult thing to face. Until now the meat had always come from a butcher, but I couldn't duck the issue, if I was prepared to buy meat from a butcher, and keep away from the reality of how that meat got there because of not facing the truth, then we should become vegetarians at once. Thinking this over for some time, and deciding that all the vegetarians we knew looked very pale and not very well, and feeling it wrong to impose this on the children, I decided to maintain our normal diet if possible. I knew virtually nothing about a vegetarian diet at that time, and felt that it would be time-consuming and difficult to cope with. Though these days I've learnt to cook quick and easy vegetarian dishes, and we have them, pretty regularly. However, I certainly could not face sending any animal of ours off in a great cattle truck to some far away abattoir, so rang an experienced goat-keeper for advice. She told me where she took hers, to a small local abattoir. It was a family firm who were most helpful to a novice, we fixed a date, and the whole thing was done humanely in my presence, so from then on it was a yearly date and the animals knew nothing about it. I owed them that.

However, little old ladies who saw the kids and lambs gambolling about used to waylay me and say, "You are going to find them good homes, aren't you?" That was very awkward, I didn't want to lie to them, but I felt sure that the truth would upset them. A good home would be with an experienced goatkeeper, possibly with room for a herd of goats, and what is needed there is a good pedigree male - not every little male goat born is required and those who think they may make charming pets, invariably do not make good homes, finding all too soon that they have bitten off more than they can chew! So in the end I said "Oh, yes." and changed the subject. The question was rather hard to take however, and surprised me from people who happily bought their meat from the butcher, and in some cases from the supermarket, and I would enquire if they were vegetarians, if so I tried to spare their feelings too. If not I explained how I felt about the big abattoirs, and why I accompanied my animals and looked after them until it was all over. I couldn't tell them why I still ate meat, but said I felt one has a duty to every living thing to see that it is humanely treated right to the end. Not wanting to upset the children, nor lie, I told them that we were like farmers now and all our male animals would have to go to the butcher, and be exchanged for other meat and then did not dwell upon the subject. These things were done when they were at school.

Chapter 13
Spring into Summer

Our first year was exceeding our expectations, it seemed to me that the children's lives were as good as one could have wished for, in spite of me being so busy in the garden and with the animals, they were able to have their friends over during the weekends and for them, goats, kids and lambs were a novelty. During the summer we could always go swimming nearby and the "lawn" which was becoming a rougher and rougher paddock was nevertheless large enough to kick a football about on, while they waited for the next meal to appear. The school too had various things on in the evenings during the week, which now we lived nearer, everyone could join in. John took up archery and David decided to learn the guitar along with a group of friends, he was interested in so much that was on offer that in his enthusiasm he occasionally double-booked! Ben and Kate in due course also put their names down for after-school activities, Ben joining the guitar group and Kate going in for five-a-side football!

Having reached that phase of parent-hood, when one becomes a taxi service, we had to work out how to co-ordinate everyone's comings and goings. It was certainly worth it though and I was very grateful that they were able to have interests, and fun, in spite of everything.

As the days grew longer, going down the garden to tend to the goats and lambs was a much more pleasurable experience. No more wrestling with binder twine on hay and straw, with frozen and painful fingers, no more slipping about with buckets of water icily sloshing into ones shoes, or coping with deluges of icy rain whilst trying to get the evening feeds to the animals in a dry condition, as the water poured down through all the gaps of one's inadequate mac. Whole days of rain at times when one had to milk and feed morning and evening, and give clean water and food mid-day as well as they couldn't go out to graze. Fancy not having to go out in that, imagine curling up in front of the fire and reading a book in the afternoon, as someone told me she did, when her two children were at school! However, in my heart of hearts I knew that once one was out in it, it was much less dreadful than looking at it from indoors, and better, far better than being tied to an office desk all day.

As imperceptibly the weather changed, and once all the children were tucked up cosily in their beds each night, the garden became a magical and peaceful place, changing from its stark winter appearance, as first snowdrops, then some daffodils rose from the sleeping earth, they were joined by a few purple crocuses and followed by primroses all over the high bank by the leat, and the long pink sprays of flowering currant. Then one amazing night, there were the frogs! Going quietly down to fetch Daisy to be milked (tied to the kitchen table with her bucket of oats); I was stopped in my tracks by a loud croak. Thunderstruck, and thinking one only heard frog choruses in the tropics, I stood and listened as the sky darkened, and more stars appeared, then the first bass frog was answered by a tenor, and then another, then more and more joining in, a constant comforting sort of growling from all around the pond, punctuated by the high bell like tones of frog sopranos, though always, now again, as if he was something very special, the deep tones of the first frog rolling out his deep satisfying roars, and so it continued throughout the evening, and many magic nights after that, right outside the goat house .

The Spring seemed to be the best time of the year for these wonderful choruses, it was a lovely accompaniment to the evenings milking and feeding jobs, and although later, after the frog spawn was to be seen floating on the surface of the pond most of the adult frogs wandered off to their various habitats around the neighbourhood, there were still our residents who lived amongst the weeds in the old rockery and they still sang occasionally as soloists, and performed duets during the summer evenings. As the weeks passed the garden revealed more of its hidden treasures - flowering cherries near the house, and a pink prunus; a wonderful red rose helped to hide the ugly, but low wall to the west, and honeysuckle entwined along it. By the front gate there blossomed a white lilac and a syringa bush, their scents lay warmly in the air and welcomed us home each evening, and cheered and nourished my soul as I faced the early morning start each day. We may have been as poor as church mice, but so rich in other ways, and a scented garden no matter how small can bring peace from worldly problems.

I was surprised one morning when the phone rang to hear Mrs. Toms the farmer's wife, she sounded busy and hurried, but had very kindly rung to say that Mary had to be shorn and would I please bring her down this morning, as the men had started the shearing. Thinking how extraordinarily kind of them it was to be taking us under their wing like this, I went to tell the family. We had by now this big leather collar which Mary wore to go up the foot-path, and I attached a dog lead to this, the boys went off to fetch Mary and put it on her, and I made the usual straw nest in the back of the mini, and fixed the "Goat-guard" up, and turned to find Mary trotting happily towards the mini with all four children as escorts. Mary Plain was quite used to climbing the back steps and coming into the kitchen, and even now and again slipped passed when we were not on the qui vive, and up the stairs, not to be encouraged now that she was more sheep-sized, than in her youth. This meant however, that hopping into the back of the mini, with Kate encouraging from within, was no big deal as far as she was concerned.

As usual when one is alone with children, what one does, everyone does, you cannot leave anybody on their own. This had always been the case and no-one thought anything of it, so of course we all set off to take Mary to be shorn. Mr. Toms, though busy seemed delighted to see all the children and Mary on her lead piling out of the car, the shearers appeared amused, and were told to be very careful with her and not nick her with their shears! Mr. Toms said she would be done immediately, and to take off her collar and lead. She was very good and submitted to this new experience without fuss, and we all enjoyed watching the shearers at work. She looked much less bulky and dignified without her wool, "Poor Mary," said John, "She looks so thin!" I was worried at the sight of the poor little thing that had emerged from all the wool, but Mr. Toms examined her knowledgeably, running his hands over her, and pronounced her to be in fine fettle, to my relief. He then asked me if I wanted the fleece which one of the men was rolling up neatly, I hadn't expected that, and said "Oh, no thanks." At which point he bought it from me. I felt rather embarrassed and didn't think that it was right that he should, but very matter-of-factly he explained that he was going to sell them all, and that I should have the money for mine. I felt it was so kind, and for the children's sake I accepted, it would help towards the inevitable holiday expenses. They all watched as Mary hopped nimbly into the back of the car again, with her entourage around her, and we drove happily home. She was very jaunty and skippy when back with the goats, and quite rejuvenated! They looked her over to make sure that it was indeed Mary, as they all went into the paddock for the rest of the morning.

As the year progressed into summer and the greenhouse was producing masses of tomatoes and cucumbers, and the garden gave us currants, red and black and white, and the beans did phenomenally well, we were incredibly lucky to find people who would buy our surplus. It was lovely of them, but it was that kind of place. To do this commercially one would have to find a market, and deliver, nothing like the way I simply offered my surplus, when it was available. Also I had no idea what anything was worth, but somehow muddled through! We had dropped off the world completely, but oh dear, there is always the electricity bill and the rates to be considered! I tried making fudge - it was delicious, and sold, but I couldn't make it cheaply enough to cover my costs and make a worthwhile profit so gave that up, along with really delicious lemon curd, just not economically viable for me.

As for the mini, it was old and now and again when things wore out, it could be a major catastrophe. Sometimes we drove with plastic containers of water to feed the radiator at intervals, no-one could find the problem, they would peek into the radiator and assure me there was plenty of water - then one day they discovered that it was in fact full of rusted particles of metal with a little water on top - no wonder she didn't like hills! More often it was brake linings that needed renewing, and tyres wore out at a phenomenal rate, but the shabby little car was our life-line, things had to be sold, and bills juggled to cover the cost. Once, we were driving home after spending a day with my mother and the mini broke down in a little country lane – worrying; no mobile telephones in those days. It was a great relief when an elderly man stopped and kindly had a look under the bonnet, he wasn't too sure, but thought he'd done something so it would get us home. After heartfelt thanks from us all, we cautiously started off, and our Good Samaritan followed us - to see us safely as far as the main road, I thought. Eventually Kate asked why he was flashing his lights, and John thought he heard his horn. We stopped - the poor man had left his spectacles under our bonnet!

On the whole one could forget ones worries in summer, the weather made everything like a holiday, and soon it really was school summer holidays when we had our meals in the garden, and spent every moment outdoors.

Luckily for me John and David had both had camping trips with their groups at school, and Ben and Kate being younger had picnic days out instead, so I felt that they had some excitement, as we couldn't possibly afford to go away, but we took picnics to the beach and swam, and all of them had invitations to spend days with their friends, or the occasional night and so on.

"Are you going on holiday this year?" People would ask, "No we couldn't possibly leave the animals!" I would nonchalantly reply. No-body understands poverty, unless they've lived it! I admire the politicians who have tried to experience it, but its pretty impossible to really find out what it is like, unless you do it until your house is damp and growing black mould up the walls as ours did in the winter, and cracks develop, and leaks appear, and paint peels etc. etc.

I actually tried to avoid having anyone to stay at first, there was no room anyway, and I didn't feel grown-up enough to cope with other people's children though friends constantly came to spend the day. Looking back at the old calendars on which I put everything from dental appointments which seemed to happen every holidays, to how many eggs were collected each day, when hay and straw were bought, when oats and corn; Vets visits, friend and relative visits to us and ours to them; when things were sown and then harvested, and the daily vegetable yields, in fact every occurrence that took place, except when time was at such a premium that I forgot! I can hardly believe how much we fitted in; I simply cannot imagine how we ever did it all! Also in due course it seemed that no-one minded about there being no room, as long as they were allowed to bring their sleeping bags and all sleep on the floor. This was a new idea for me, but I had to give in, and everyone seemed delighted with the arrangement, so we did that very occasionally when they got a bit older, as I didn't honestly think we could afford it.

Those summers were wonderful, once winter was over the sun shone; it seemed to me, right through till autumn came round again. There must have been some rain occasionally, though I remember watering the vegetables and the greenhouse regularly once a week giving everything a good soaking by dipping my watering-can into the stream on the end of a rope and hauling it up when full.

I remember one summer holiday when

John and David decreed the garden pond ought to be emptied and cleaned, and all four of them in bathing things with buckets and bits of old hose-pipe, emptying it out and then coming across an eel they had caught one autumn when our kind neighbour Mr. Goode had explained how to catch them as they went up-river past the garden!! They had not forgotten his words, and had gone down one evening and putting into practice what they had been told, actually caught one! "It was quite small," said David, "Just a baby one!" John added as they came dashing in for supper that evening delighted at their success. "What did you do with it?" I asked. "Put it in the pond!" was the answer.

I used to look for it occasionally, but there was never a sign of it, we knew that eels can cross land and assumed it must have found its way back over the grass to the stream quite easily. So a year or two later it had grown quite a bit, and caused a lot of excitement, four figures in bathing suits tore past me, and returned in record time, now wearing wellies for protection, "Quick, get a bucket!" yelled someone. Luckily we had a big black plastic one in the greenhouse and it was eventually caught and transported back to the stream and released, to my relief!

I had been saving every penny I could in all directions throughout the year and sold one of the last pieces of jewellery in order to buy a chest freezer, which could be housed in the garage, this was for all the surplus milk produced during the summer, we could use it when the yield went down during the winter. This year we could freeze our runner beans instead of salting them - much nicer, also vegetables and fruit. I planned to do batches of cooking as well and have extra stews and Shepherds Pies, Fish Pies, Cheese Flans and cakes in the freezer for when time was short, or something unexpected happened. This worked up to a point, if one didn't have to buy any extra ingredients, and used mainly one's own produce. These days my shopping list seldom varied from the basics, as we produced as much as possible and cooked each week, for the week.

One of the traditions we had every summer was to spend the day at our local "Show" every town and village seems to have one, though village ones are generally fetes. For weeks before, where-ever you go some-one is sure to say "Going to the Show then?" You would feel terribly out of it if you weren't. The Show is something we all loved, and at ours the weather was always wonderful, it was the proud boast of the Mayor that it never rained on that day, and it never did until the children were grown-up!!!

We tried to get there in good time, to get a convenient parking place, and as usual there was a horse show, and a dog show, and pens of sheep and cattle to visit, and several big marquees. The first we entered had every kind of Cockerel and hen; and in the next children were showing their family pets - hamsters, guinea pigs, and rabbits, and one little boy had a cock and hen of his own, he stroked them lovingly as he told us about them, he was certainly going into farming!

The handicrafts varied from home-made fudge, to smocks in bright colours, leather goods, woven and knitted garments, jewellery, and stuffed toys. It was unbelievably hot in the marquees, so we looked at the outside stalls in between each one. Granny had given each child some money last time we had seen her, and this was saved for today; so John and David each had a go with a mallet in trying to make a bell ring, and Ben and Kate went to see who could throw a wellie the furthest, but it was when David tried throwing a dart into a row of cards that things got more exiting - he got an Ace at his first attempt, and came away delightedly carrying a goldfish in a plastic bag, to my relief he ended up selling it to someone at school, who knew a bit about keeping such things!

He had a good eye and a steady hand, and could always be relied on to get a dart into a winning number, or a golf ball into a hole, and as the years went by I used to beg him not to win any livestock, after he won a pig at a village fete, which we had to give back as I couldn't possibly cope with it at the time!

"Phew, said Ben, "I am so hot!" "And thirsty," Kate added. As I knew we couldn't afford to buy lunch we had a picnic waiting in the car, so made our way back there and ate our hard-boiled eggs, and salad sandwiches in the shade at the side of it, quenching our thirst with home-made lemonade, before going back to watch the riders taking the horses over jumps, and doing various stunts, including a fancy dress parade, which was won by a little boy with a cherubic face dressed as a sweep, riding a donkey and carrying a sweeps brush, his face was blackened, and he wore a tatty old coat with the sleeves turned back, also judiciously blackened, and his sister's trousers, (his having been left at home in the rush), while she sat crossly in the car! We were nearby and felt for her!

Later we wandered on to a smaller ring

where we found goats being judged. They looked lovely, white British Saanens like Daisy, Toggenburgs - black and white with little toggles hanging under their chins, and the lovely Anglo-Nubians, brown with beautiful hanging down ears (not for beginners, we'd been told). After that there was an announcement that tea was being served over in a corner of the big field, and that later that evening a band would be providing music for dancing late into the evening in the big ring. Time to go home for us, but as we walked through one big tent on our way to the car-park, to our delight we met an enchanting looking Llama called Angel, she was quiet and dainty with huge long eye-lashes, she turned and looked at us, we looked adoringly back, then, "Don't get too close," said her owner, "I'm afraid she spits!

After a day out we generally spent the next one at home, that is in the garden and taking the animals up the footpath to graze without the need to bring them back early. The children liked playing in the little wood along the footpath which was fine, I could hear their voices, and see them too if I looked out of the window, or up from the hoeing. Then we'd eat in the garden, and maybe have a swim about tea-time after bringing the goats home.

As Mary always came back early we had to rig up some shade for her in the "paddock". How to do that was a puzzle, until I thought of our old garden parasol, it was very bright and garish and we never used it, now that at our end of the garden we had the little cherry trees to give us shade. So we tied it firmly to one of the fence posts, and when she came home before lunch, she would make straight for the gate of the paddock, wait to be let in, and after a drink from her bucket, would flop down in her shady spot in complete contentment. Generally at that time of the year when she returned she would have a bemused holiday-maker in tow, hanging on to the end of her lead. There would be a banging on the back-door, and when I opened it "Is she yours?" someone would enquire, "I met her trotting along, and didn't like to leave her, but she seemed to know where she was going and led me in here!" "Oh yes," I'd explain, "She knows exactly what to do, she was just coming home as she'd had enough grazing!" I thanked them very much for being so kind and they told Mary she was a very intelligent sheep, and watched with great amusement as she made her way into the paddock and flopped down under her sunshade.

One day towards the end of the summer

holidays David remarked rather wistfully that we never went to the old haunts anymore, "Well, it's rather far and an awful waste of petrol/money when we have a good beach just half a mile away here." "I'd like to go!" said Kate, "So would I!" Ben added. "Just once!" said John. So remembering the fleece money, it was agreed. "If you all help bring the animals home later, I will have time to get a picnic organised." I said.

Before bed-time every-one sorted out their fishing rods for the expedition, while I was getting the supper, corn-beef pie from the freezer, popped into the oven till piping hot served with coleslaw, and our own raspberries for pud, everyone's favourite and quick to prepare.

For the picnic we could have cheese flan in wholemeal pastry, hard-boiled eggs, and a salad with lettuce, tomatoes, cucumber, and sliced beetroot, with a banana to finish, and home-made lemonade to drink, this was a favourite with everyone and so economical for picnics, or when anyone came to visit, as we normally just drank water throughout the day. Just half a lemon whizzed up in a liquidizer full of water, strained, add sugar to taste and Bob's your uncle!

Next day after bringing the animals back

from grazing in time for us to get to our old beach for lunch, we set off, reminiscing as we went. "Do you remember when we ran out of petrol on the way to school, just as we slid into the garage?" asked John as we passed it. "Remember, Godfrey and Fraser?" asked David as we entered the lane where we always saw them on the way home from school, two dear old men taking an elderly dog for a walk, each day the same walk, the same time. We used to wave to them, and David named them after two Dad's Army characters, as he thought they looked exactly like them! "I remember Daisy jumping over that gate!" said Ben, "And I remember the rats in the farmers barn," said Kate, "and you boys trying to shoot them with your toy bows and arrows!" "There weren't really rats were there?" I asked in horror. "Yes there were." came the emphatic answer. I'd thought it all a game, truly a case of ignorance is bliss! "There's the sea!" I pointed out, "Shall I let you out at the footpath to run down, like you used to?" So out they all poured, and I followed the road down, meeting them at the bottom as they hurtled down the path to race the car.

Of course it was absolutely necessary to swim before lunch, as one had to wait two hours after eating before swimming again, in case of cramp. John and David however had their hearts set on fishing today, so only Ben and Kate went in and I thought it was really rather cool for swimming, so although I put on my bathing dress in case of having to rescue anyone, I had a lazy time on the beach and watched with Delilah till everyone had had enough and came ravening up the beach for food! The wind was freshening and we decided to go up the path and eat lunch on the grass, sheltered by bushes and bramble patches. Here it was hot and blissful, and we munched hungrily, watching the waves climbing up the beach; they seemed to be getting noisier and foamier as they came. A white piece of paper or plastic washed in and out with each wave, was that a wing flapping about? It must be a dead gull, David saw it too and putting down his egg rushed off to investigate. He returned carrying a little Black-headed gull in his arms! Quite alive but rather bemused it regarded us all calmly. We examined it carefully; there were no injuries, nothing to explain its predicament. We stood it on the grass and it wobbled weakly and then sank down on the turf and there it sat. "Oh dear! Let's wrap it up and get it dry and warm in the smallest towel, and then see how it is before we go home." I said, so there it sat on the grass beside us, with just its head peering out of its cocoon, as we continued lunch, with no sign of nervousness and apparently quite content to be there.

When it was time to go home, we unwrapped it and set it upon its legs, I hoped it would immediately take to its wings, but it simply sat down again after a wobbly few moments, and didn't attempt so much as a single step away from us! There was nothing for it but to wrap it up in its towel again and take it home, with us. We would have to stop in the little town en route to get some fish, and luckily arrived before they closed and were able to park right outside - they had no small fish, but I got some fillets which we could cut up into small slivers.

When we got home it was panic stations, to get the gull settled in, supper cooked, children to bed and goats milked, before it got too late. Not for the first time I thanked my lucky stars that I never threw anything away; in the garage was an old tea-chest that had come from my mother, the boys fetched it and we set it up on its side in the corner at the far end of the living/dining-room, where it wouldn't be disturbed. We fitted it up with newspapers on the floor, and plastic sheeting under it, and a nest of straw in the corner. We gave it a deep pot of drinking water wedged in the front of the chest, and then offered our guest some bits of fish - to our delight it daintily accepted a few pieces, we left some more in a bowl near its water, and then popped it gently onto its nest at the back of the chest, we had a rigid piece of wire mesh left over from fence building, - what it was meant for originally, no-one knew, but it was big enough to wedge against the front of the chest to keep the gull safely inside for the night.

Next morning there was the little figure standing up, albeit rather shakily, in the front of its new home looking calmly out at us. David gave it its fish, and clean water, and after breakfast, I renewed its carpet of papers. So for some time David tended his charge which he named "Bird", morning and evening. It showed no desire to fly, but seemed better and less weak each day. "If only we could let it out to stretch its legs, but how to protect the carpet?" I wondered. John climbed into the attic, he and David were the only two who could, they were always able to somehow do the impossible and reach ceiling height, push open the trap-door and return with something to solve the current problem; this time it was a large plastic sheet which he'd discovered when exploring before. (The children firmly believed that Treasure was to be found in attics, and loved to be allowed to climb into Granny's attic for a treat, so naturally our own had been checked out at an early stage!) This had clearly once been around a new mattress - very useful! We spread it out all over that end of the room, covered it with a thick mat of newspapers, and Bird was happy to approve. Also that is where he remained, not walking far without sinking down for a rest. Delilah accepted his presence without comment, and showed no interest in the proceedings. If we went out in the afternoon we simply popped him back in his cage for safety with clean water and a little extra fish.

Eventually it dawned on me that we didn't know if Bird's feathers were water-tight, he'd seemed to be drowning when found, and if someone had rescued him as a bird covered in oil, cleaned him up and released him before his feathers had recovered their natural buoyancy, then that would account for his tameness and condition perhaps. "We'll have to fill the bath for him, and see how he copes!" I announced, Ben went off to turn it on and fill it from the cold tap. Then David picked up Bird, but as we made for the stairs Bird began to struggle, until as David stood still for him, Bird made his way onto David's head and there he stood regally, if slightly rockily until they reached the bathroom, and was lowered and manoeuvred gently onto the water.

If only I had a camera I thought, as we all stood and delighted in the sight of our own live bath toy as he floated there serenely looking around at us. "Let's see if he'll fish!" said John and fetched some bits, but Bird let them sink to the bottom. He seemed quite buoyant however, and just as we were about to bring him out he started to bathe. That was a bit splashy, but a very good sign we felt. Finally David tried to pick him up but that seemed to make him a bit panicky, so we hung a bath towel over the edge of the bath and the little bird scrabbled up that with David's help, he stood on the bath mat for a few minutes to preen, and was then transported on David's head back to his home in the chest. From then on we made this a daily routine, always with Bird travelling regally up on David's head. We thought the whole process was helping him exercise and get stronger as he began to paddle about gently and always bathed. When I was able to get some sprats, I cut small silvery slivers, and threw them in and he grabbed a few before they went down. Another good sign we thought, and when the bath was filled to the brim and an old piece of towelling hung over the edge, Bird was able to scrabble out with a bit of flapping by himself when he was ready.

The day finally came when coming into the sitting-room from the kitchen, I found Bird standing on the narrow window-sill, facing south. He was just gazing out, then quite gently he rose in the air and flew the length of the room to the Northern window, and round and back, landing neatly in his run. I gave him some fish, and decided that in a day or two, once we were sure that he could fly strongly we must take him back from whence he came. Most wild birds want only to escape, but Bird was totally unique, it was a mystery.

A day or two later he was flying strongly, it was wonderful to see, so graceful, probably because he was in no sort of panic about it, the following morning Bird showed impatience to be let out of the chest for the first time, and promptly flew the length of the room. When we were in the garden with the animals we heard him tapping at the window and knew the time had come, he wanted to get out, and go home. We discussed the release of Bird over tea, "Ohhh! Can't we keep him?" asked Kate, but we talked about wild things belonging to themselves, not to us, and explained that once he was strong he wouldn't be happy here, he needed to be with his own kind.

After everyone had talked it over, we made a plan to take him back to the beach in the morning after the goat chores, if the weather forecast was alright. Thank goodness it was set fair for a few days, soon the summer would be over and he needed to get going now. So the following morning we set off as soon as possible, with our picnic, water for Delilah, and Bird, this time in a covered basket, so he could feel independent, and it was probably safer now that he was fit again, one did not want him trying to fly or struggle in the car.

There were very few people about on the beach today, for which I was truly grateful. John carried the basket and walked along towards the middle of the beach where there were flocks of seagulls, we got as near as possible without making them take flight. "Ben will you pick up Delilah and hold her, so she doesn't start chasing seagulls?" "Kate, you and I, and John must spread out in case Bird doesn't make it, we will have to try and catch him again." Privately I prayed fervently that he would, as I thought our chances of recapturing him were pretty forlorn, and I didn't want the children upset if it all went wrong. "John, just open the lid a little way, so David can pick Bird out, and then David you must hold him neatly in your hands and then just gently whoosh him up into the air, once he has got his bearings!"

Off went Bird, circled once and landed on the sea where he bathed and bathed, it was rather worrying as it went on so long, would he get water-logged even after our precautions with the daily bath, and start drowning again? Then from the middle of the flock beside us rose another small gull, it flew out and landed near Bird, bathed a bit and then bobbed about companionably, when it arose to fly back so did Bird, they both alighted amongst all the others and we lost sight of them, but we felt that all was well. We took Delilah away from temptation, now that Bird was no longer a member of the family! Further back along the beach, everyone had a swim before lunch, we kept looking but there was no sign of Bird being in any kind of trouble so eventually we made our way home, me with a great sense of relief. "I wonder if he will fly over our garden one day!" said David. A few days later a small dainty gull with did indeed appear wheeling over our garden - who knows?

Chapter 14

Parsley

Daisy's female kid had grown up healthy and strong, the father had been a pedigree Saanen goat from a good line, as dear Daisy was really an unregistered little scrub goat with rather peculiarly shaped udders, it seemed a good idea to try to improve her descendants through careful breeding. Parsley appeared to be a great success; she was much larger than Daisy and to my untutored eyes looked pretty good. However, there was no getting away from it she did not have her mother's intelligence, she would stand on your toes without a seconds thought and make no attempt to move away, this was very painful as she was extremely heavy, "Get off Parsley!" someone would cry urgently, pushing her away, this was easier said than done, as she would just lean against the push, or look bemused. Keeping goats probably teaches one to be gentle and patient, more than most things, rather like cats they have minds of their own, and must sometimes be managed with a certain amount of guile and tact. It was as well in the case of Parsley, not to stand in her way as you were quite liable to fall over if she accidentally barged into you sideways on. Nevertheless, like Daisy she had a nice nature, just seemed rather a galumph, not what one expects from a dainty creature like a goat!

Before the end of the holidays we noticed that the Goat Society were having a show at a village not far from my mother's house, and we all thought it would be fun to have a go at showing her. She would be judged according to her points, and it would be useful to see how she measured up in the goat world, it was advertised as an informal family occasion, with things happening for the children to enjoy, "Can your goat find its owner?!", being something that sounded rather fun.

I felt a bit shy about it but every-one else was very keen, and it sounded like a relaxed and informal event. We looked at Parsley with a critical eye, would she do? Luckily I had trimmed the goats' hooves after the last shower of rain, so they were in good condition. Once I had discovered about hoof trimming I did them religiously once a month, when Daisy had first come to us hers were pretty neglected and I had to wait until she kidded to attend to them. I found it a nerve racking job at first, but both the goats and I had got used to it with practice, as it is an essential part of goat-keeping. I rang a goat-keeping friend for advice and she suggested that a few days before the show, we should wash Parsley with Baby shampoo, but on no account get her too wet, on account of her thin skin, and danger of a chill, and we should dry her well, she looked so lovely and white it seemed to be gilding the lily, but wanting to do the right thing we tied her up on the lawn and proceeded with luke-warm water to shampoo her and rinse her with a cloth keeping her from getting too wet! It was a hot day or I probably wouldn't have dared risk it, but she took it all in her stride. The day before the show she looked lovely, but unfortunately on her way up the garden and feeling a little peckish she made a bee-line for a small Schumacher tree by the wall, grabbed a branch and proceeded to chew it up, giving herself a strange black mark on her lips! I rushed for a damp cloth and did my best to clean her up, most of it came off, all except one smudge that looked pretty awful, I didn't want to put soap on her mouth so hoped it would be gone by morning.

Next day was bright and sunny with a light breeze, we did the chores, and loaded the back of the mini with nice clean straw for Parsley to lie on, and hay in case she felt peckish. This time we left Delilah at home for once, feeling that we did not know how she would behave surrounded by strange goats and perhaps other dogs. Ben checked that her water bowl was clean and full, and left a few dog-biscuits for her, she normally turned up her nose at such things, but being on her own she might need something to do when not snoozing in her basket.

I had to push my nervousness aside, and not let the children know my misgivings, I wanted them to have a good time. What was I doing though, taking a novice goat to a show, being a complete novice myself?!! Mad! I had read up all I could, but that was not exactly reassuring, however the various goat-keepers that I had met so far were unfailingly nice kind people, and there was no backing out now! We disposed the picnic, a container of water and bucket for Parsley's drink, around everyone's feet, we checked that the dog-guard - now called a goat-guard - was firm and safe, everyone piled in, and we were off. It was a lovely day, the sky was a limitless blue, with just a few small white clouds, the sun was warm, and summer was disinclined to depart just yet! The dear little winding lanes led us away into the deeper countryside, Parsley munched tranquilly in the back, and everyone began to sing. Eventually, rounding a corner we got a view as the lane dropped away ahead, of a wood, and beyond that a tall slim church spire, this must be our first view of the village we were aiming for, and sure enough sooner than expected we came upon a large field entrance, parked cars within, and marquees, and of course goats. Children ran about or walked their charges and there were lots of people looking very professional in white coats! Oh, dear we didn't have one of those!

I parked the car at the end of a row, and we looked for the place where we had to register Parsley's name, "There it is". John pointed it out, "Further up the hill." I locked the car and slid the window open by Parsley's nose to give her air, and we all trooped off to find out what we had to do. "We've never done this before", I explained and the nice girl in charge of the entries, gave me a form to fill in. "What breed?" she asked. As I handed it back. "British Saanen." I replied knowledgeably. "Oh!" the girl laughed amusedly "Is that her?" I was just about to explain that No, she was in the car, when the children all gasped "Parsley!" Looking around in horror, I beheld our goat, galumphing up the field in search of us! Oh the shame of it! Every other goat in the place was quietly standing behind a tiny piece of string, a barrier, which would not have detained any of mine for a micro-second, or lying quietly and tidily near its owners' car on a neat lead, or walking beside its young owner as if butter wouldn't melt. While ours looking larger than life was hurtling about in wild abandon, calling desperately! Feeling as if all eyes were upon us we all ran to the rescue! Daisy had always been quite contented to lie in the car and wait for us; it had never occurred to me that Parsley would not do the same.

We discovered that she had put her nose in the gap and simply continued to push the window right back, whereupon she had somehow squeezed herself through, luckily without hurting herself in any way. Mortified I decided that I would have to stay with her until her class came up, and suggested that the four children went off and explored the show without me. "When you get back we'll have some lunch, and be already to take her into the ring!" I said with a lot more confidence than I felt, we could do without any more shame-making performances! Eventually when they all returned, I tied Parsley firmly to one of the Mini's door handles, with some food and water strategically placed just within her reach, and we settled ourselves on the grass, just out of her reach to have our picnic.

It was while Ben was telling me about the other goats he'd seen being shown, that he suddenly stopped mid-stream, "Who is going into the ring with Parsley?" he asked. We all looked at each other, - then "I am." Kate calmly announced. "She is my goat, I'll take her round!" She was eight years old now, Parsley had been born the day after her birthday, and somehow we had forgotten that Kate obviously thought that this had been Daisy's gift to her. "Perhaps, John should do it as he's the eldest." I suggested as tactfully as possible. Kate looked at me, as always so small and dainty, always neat in her jeans, with her hair gently curling round her face, big hazel eyes, and rose-petal skin, how could this little thing cope with the galumphing Parsley? Ha! One look at that determined expression made it seem highly probable that she could and would! Besides in truth no-one else was that keen, not now that we had seen the pristine white coats, and quiet and perfectly mannered goats. So with the rest of us at the ringside, ready to duck in and help if necessary, she led Parsley into the ring after the others, then a nice judge standing in the centre went over to her and explained that she should stand on the opposite side of her goat, and then just do what the others did. Parsley knew she had met her match, and behaved so well that to everyone's utter astonishment and jubilation she won second prize. The kind judge came over to us afterwards and explained that she would have, in fact, been awarded the first prize for her quality had she not had the black stain on her lips!! So of course we told her all about how it came to be there, and how I had been afraid to harm her by taking it off, and we received several helpful tips in return, for next time!

When we called in at Gran's house on the way home and had tea in the garden, with Parsley judiciously tethered in a safe place nearby, she was highly amused to hear of Kate's triumph at winning a red rosette with her goat! When we eventually arrived home again, Kate went straight down to the goat-house and tied the Rosette to a strong nail sticking out of a beam over Parsley's stall. The first of many perhaps! Next morning with a wail of frustration, she discovered that Parsley took after Daisy in reaching impossible heights, and had taken down her rosette and eaten it in the night - apart from a microscopic piece still attached to the nail!

As the holidays drew to a close, like squirrels we began to harvest our produce for the winter. Throughout the summer, once the children were in bed I had picked unlimited Runner Beans, it was amazing how well they grew, some to eat, some to freeze in our new freezer, and often plenty more to sell. With the Broad Beans, and French Beans, we had more than enough to eat ourselves, and then there were lovely little beetroot and lettuces, and radishes too. In August we picked delicious Victoria Plums from our little Plum Tree, this was a wonderful treat and we ate them instead of puddings. By October there were still tomatoes to be picked, and dumped in plastic bags in the freezer where they froze like billiard balls. They were easy to peel when defrosted and could be heated up to have on toast, put in cooked dishes or made into delicious soup to drink with cheese sandwiches. It was wonderful digging up our own carrots and storing them in wooden boxes begged from the grocer or one of our tea-chests. In those days one put peat around them, now I know better and would use a substitute, or straw.

We had potatoes too and did the same with them, and tried to make ropes of onions to hang from the rafters; it seems to fulfil a primeval need, filling ones store-cupboard, and preparing for the onset of winter. Luckily we had a large garage where everything went, including the goats food, and hay and straw as well as the deep freeze itself, all raised off the ground on planks of wood laid on bricks, or a wooden pallet we'd been given. The boys had found an apple tree, gone wild in the wood, so we used its windfalls to make our blackberry and apple jelly, keeping our own precious apples to stew and for Dorset Apple Cakes, and Pies. We had one wonderful tree, which produced huge apples; they weighed about a pound each! Nobody knew what the name of it was! Unfortunately hens lay fewer and fewer eggs in the winter months, and goats give less and less milk, but we had frozen some of our milk to see us through and while the yield was still up, made cakes and puddings, and cheese flans, and white sauce, and cheese sauce for delicious Cauliflower Cheese suppers with mashed potatoes.

The last thing we did every summer holiday was go back to our beach with a picnic, it was the best place to find lots of blackberries too, so when possible I picked for our usual bramble jelly whilst there. Sometimes it was warm enough for a swim, sometimes we just ran along the beach, and once it was so rough with huge waves pounding on the shore, that it was really rather frightening and calling to the family to keep back from the water's edge I racked my brains to think of an excuse to get them away to safety. At that very moment I saw David bend down and grab something and they all came hurtling back in great excitement, the wind blew the words away, as they shouted and waved their arms about, then "A fish - it was a fish - did you see!" They were all talking at once, eyes shining with the joy of it. "Mum," shouted David against the wind, "This fish came flying through the air - straight out of a huge wave, and landed at my feet!" "I thought he'd lose it!" said John in amazement, "The wave came right up the beach after it!" "Let me see, let me see!" Ben and Kate were bouncing up and down, trying to get a good look at it. "I can't believe it, I never heard of such a thing!" I said in amazement, but there it was, a very lively fish in David's arms. "We need a priest!" said John. "That's the thing you use to kill a fish with." Ben explained to me kindly. The boys took charge, and despatched the fish so we could take it home for me to cook!

Chapter 15
Toast

When the children go back to school in the autumn, it is a happy occasion, as are all the beginnings. We all love the start of the holidays and celebrate each season as it comes, at least I do, and so of course do they but not consciously. At the end of each holiday where I expected a sadness, there was none, they looked forward to seeing their friends again and all the things they could do outside the curriculum - camping, swimming, picnics or parties, canoeing or climbing, or the school play or concert - in season, while I enjoyed the change of routine each time as well; now we could begin to look forward to fires in the grate, hot-buttered toast for tea with curtains pulled against the dark outside, and the cosiness of winter evenings.

One morning after leaving the children at school, I got home just as the telephone rang, it was Mrs. Toms to say her husband wanted me to take Mary down right away to be dipped. Dipped!? Mary!? Surely not, "Oh how kind of him, but I don't think I'll bother to have her dipped!" I innocently replied. Poor Mrs. Toms she sounded really worried as she explained that it really had to be done, it was the law that all sheep had to go through this process. "Oh I see, of course, I'll bring her down now, and thank-you so very much for letting me know!" and I dashed down the garden with her collar and lead to fetch her. She hopped happily into the back of the mini, and settled down behind the goat-guard like an old hand, and off we went. It was all go down at the farm, with several men manning the dip and the sheep all filing through, and being flung into the strong smelling liquid. Someone pushed them under one by one, and then out they scrambled to drain off. I felt sorry for Mary. "We'll do her next." Mr. Toms ordained, explaining to the others that she was a tame sheep! (Always more difficult, with minds of their own, apparently). She certainly couldn't be shooed in, however she was very good considering. I took off her lead, and Mr. Toms managed to man-handle her in, a quick dip and out she came, I popped her lead back on, and had to wait a bit for her to drain, as gallons of the stuff poured off, before letting her leap with alacrity back into the safety of her car and taking her home.

In later years Mr. Toms offered to keep

her after dipping and let her run with the ram, instead of me having to bring her down again for her nuptials in November when she had to be left for a week or so with the flock and ram. This first year, when we took her back just before Guy Fawkes, he kept her there over the winter, but the children missed her, and wanted to see her before Christmas, so Mr. Toms took us to the field where she was indistinguishable amongst the rest of the flock, however Kate started calling her and out came Mary from the centre of them all and trotted over to be kissed, I wondered if she would want to come home with us, but we all stood there talking, and Mary decided to go back with the others and so we left her there, till the Spring.

As the weather got colder I searched for wood for our fire during the day, and collected boughs of greenery, from hedge trimming, and Ivy from the woods to take to the goats in their stable. Now that they were company for each other Daisy no longer accompanied me, so I would take them up the footpath to find what they could, and then brought greenery home for them to enjoy. The kind people at the greengrocers, where I bought potatoes, and vegetables when ours ran out, let us have bags of greens which they were throwing out, and outside leaves which had been trimmed off things, and carrots which were past their best etc during the winter months which helped a lot.

Delilah was a constant companion in or out of the house, and loved visits to the woods. As winter drew on however, she became ill and I took her to a local vet whom we did not know, he gave her pills, but she only became worse, he then removed her womb and we hoped so much that all would now be well, but she seemed worse than ever, so finally I took her back to our old vet who'd always looked after our goats, he tried all he could but in the end it became obvious that we should let her go. She had always been such a happy little dog; it was not fair to let the quality of her life deteriorate in this way. I stayed with her loving her and talking cheerily to her till it was over, and kept a stiff upper lip until I was in the car, where-upon I drove off with the tears pouring down my face past caring who saw, though hoping nobody noticed. I had to pull myself together before arriving at school to collect the children, and managed it for their sake, though it was very hard to break the news to them, but we agreed that it was kinder for Delilah than to keep her, selfishly, because we couldn't bear to let her go. Thinking of her we naturally began to share our memories of her, they were all happy ones, she had been there for all of Kate's life and had been a tremendous companion to us all. She was such a complete member of the family, that for days afterwards, I was still moving about as if she was by my feet, but now it was just me alone in the house, once everyone was at school, apart from the two goats and chickens, outside, and the whole place felt empty, and cheerless.

When the weather was cold and grey, or the rain coursed down outside, and the goats remained cosily in their stalls, with their food and water distributed, I would put my quilted dressing-gown on over my clothes, and sit at the dining-room table writing my stories, sometimes in the depths of winter with a hot water bottle on my lap as well!! All too soon it was time to fetch the children, and I would have to pack it all away until the next time that there might be a moment to spare! Then I could put the central heating on so the house would warm up, and be warm and welcoming by the time we got back.

Once out of the car they would all rush about the garden to let off a bit of steam before following me into the house, and one night, John announced that he'd seen a black cat in the garden. "We couldn't get near it though!"

said David rather disappointedly. "Perhaps one of the neighbours has got a new cat!" said Ben. "I didn't see it!" said Kate "Where was it?" "Don't pick it up, it must be new here, and is exploring its territory." I said, as they all went out again to find it. But it had vanished.

It was days later when David said "I saw the black cat just now, just sitting looking at us from the bank across the stream!" and again when the rest of the family went out to see it, it had vanished. At the weekend Ben said he'd seen it under a bush by the garage, so this time we all went down very quietly, but no sign of any cat! Then one evening Kate announced with satisfaction that she had at last seen the cat down at the end of the garden, and it had stayed quite still while she talked to it, but vanished into the bushes when she went to stroke it. It seemed as though the cat was introducing itself cautiously to each child, one by one, it seemed very odd that I'd never seen it, being there all day long going about doing my chores. Was it real, was it watching us, what was going on? Finally however, it was my turn! Coming out of the garage at dusk on my own one evening, across the garden one patch of darkness seemed more solid than the rest, I stared and suddenly two amber eyes blinked at me! I walked slowly towards it, but there was no cat it had simply melted away!

I had to get to the bottom of this, it so when my nearest neighbour next came out into her garden, I waylaid her, and asked if she had seen a mysterious black cat about the place. "Oh yes!" said she matter-of-factly, "I think its hungry, I offered it some bread and it ate it all! I've asked around the neighbourhood, but no-one seems to know anything about it! It does seem very timid, as though it has not been well-treated."

After that I kept my eyes peeled hoping to be able to help the poor little thing, especially as the weather was getting more wintry by the day. One evening, I again beheld the small dark figure sitting on the grass like a tea-cosy; she was watching me, as if she knew I would be going to shut up the hens, before the fox came visiting. Hardly daring to walk towards her, in case she ran, I gained her side, and sank down onto my knees beside her, whereupon she actually climbed onto my lap as light and soft as thistle-down, amazingly she clasped my wrist gently between her two soft paws, in a fleeting embrace before instantly moving away. I invited her back to the house, and fetched the last slice of meat out of the fridge, cut it into small pieces and put it on Delilah's little enamel dish, after warming it up slightly under the hot tap. I had to put it near the door for her, but that was not safe enough I suppose, as she did the most astonishing thing. Getting hold of the rim in her teeth, she dragged it over the door sill, down the two steps and then settled on the grass by a small fir tree to eat. Sitting on the steps to keep her company I tried to persuade her in, without any luck, though she sat beside me companionably for a short while. I had to come in, and when I looked out again, she had disappointingly gone.

Next morning we were getting breakfast when someone saw the desperate little face of the cat peeping nervously through the glass door. David opened it and the cat retreated instantly to a safe distance, but didn't actually vanish this time. John got Delilah's dish, and I, with nothing left to offer got an egg from the fridge which I quickly whisked up with a little milk. Kate and Ben were talking to it through the door, but it came no nearer though clearly desperate for food, so we put the dish out on the step and stood back. Very hesitantly the little cat came up the steps, and began to lap, keeping a wary eye on us meanwhile. We all hardly dared breathe, but most of the egg had gone before something startled her, and she was gone - not to be seen for the rest of the day.

It was breakfast time again when she next

appeared, and this time I had hopefully bought some proper cat-food, Kate opened the door very gently and Ben put the dish down, just inside this time, we all stood back and waited, Kate gently called and eventually a hesitant soft paw came over the threshold, she sniffed the dish, and the children were all electrified when carefully manoeuvring the edge of the dish into her mouth the little cat half carried and half dragged it out onto the top step, where she at last began to eat, at least she was staying a bit nearer now. Our hearts went out to her, so hoping fervently that she would come again we carefully made a plan. I bought more cat-food that day, and it was waiting in the kitchen with the dish, and opener beside it just in case.

If she reappeared the whole family would go into action! John would open the tin and put out some of the meat, David would put the plate a little further in than before, then they'd all stand back in full view, while Ben let her in and Kate talked gently to encourage it. I'd hide behind the door ready to close it once she was safely inside.

At last, all went according to plan, I closed the door half expecting her to go mad with fear, but no, she looked round once and then - began her meal! The relief was enormous, and as we studied the little dark figure, we realised that she wasn't black at all, but a wonderful deep colour, a mixture of black and mahogany, here and there her long fur was tipped with gold, her eyes were amber, and her soft and silent paws were surprisingly large. In spite of having lived rough for some time she was very composed and neat in her manner. When she had finished her meal we offered her a saucer of goats milk, and she daintily sipped a little of that, and then sat calmly cleaning her whiskers, while someone rescued the toast from under grill. Which was how she came to be named Toast, her coat being the sort of mottled colours, our toast had gone, each time she had appeared at breakfast time!

We all seemed to have come to the decision that she should find a home with us if she wanted one, (though later I felt that the decision had been hers). Probably she had watched us carefully during the preceding days, before introducing herself to each in turn, and our reactions being approved of, though still nervous, once she had made the decision to come in it merely signalled our welcome when I closed the door. We did our best to remember to move quietly and gently till she was used to us, and she seemed content to allow everyone to gently stroke her and talk to her. We remembered the rule, "little and often" for feeding starving creatures, until she got a bit heavier; her fur made it difficult to judge how thin she must have been. Someone gave her a cushion to sit on out of any draughts, and I rigged up a cat-litter tray, with a cardboard box, plastic and cinders, till I could get the right thing from the local pet shop, later that day. Having finally overcome her fear, and moved in, she refused to go out at all for some days, perhaps she was afraid we would not let her come back, but in due course she felt confident enough to go in and out quite happily.

After breakfast we had to coax her to come into the rest of the house, and uncertainly at first and then with more confidence she explored the big sitting room, though unless we were in there too, or whenever we went out she would repair to the sixth step of the stairs, where she stayed - apparently keeping an eye on the front door till we returned, she wouldn't go any further up. And for the first few days that is where she spent most of her time, until evening came and we persuaded her to come into the sitting-room with us, when she would curl up on the sofa or the arm-chair apparently content. I wondered often where she had come from and formed the idea that she had belonged to an old lady perhaps, she was so gentle and dainty in her manner, maybe a young family had taken her on who hadn't really liked cats, had frightened her and had not allowed her upstairs, who knows, anyway she had fallen on hard times, and had forgotten how to purr. When I noticed this silence I wondered if she was dumb.

When you have animals with children, of course you have to worm them periodically, and so Toast was treated early on, for safety's sake A few days later Kate had to stay in bed with a feverish cold, and announced that she wanted Toast to keep her company, without thinking I went onto the landing and called "Toast", how foolish, she won't know her name yet, I thought, but "mew?" came enquiringly from the hall, I looked over the banisters, "Toast, come on, clever girl!" and "Kitty, kitty, kitty!" to make certain, she knew she was welcome. Light as a feather she silently ran up the stairs, and followed me into Kate's room, I lifted her onto the bed and she settled down as Kate stroked her gently. Then Kate was startled as the little cat started kneading her dressing-gown with her furry paws, and sucking the edge, it's alright I told her, poor little thing was probably taken away from her mother too soon, and never had enough sucking, so Kate, reassured, continued lovingly stroking the little cat trying to make up for the bad times she had been through, and Toast lay there looking blissful. Half-way down the stairs to get on with the housework, I suddenly heard purring, - great incredibly loud rolls of purring, it seemed as if the whole house reverberated with her comforting contented purrs.

Now when I sat and wrote Toast would often sit on my lap, and on winter evenings when the children were asleep, and the goats chores finished, there was a warm house, a fire to sit beside, and a cosy purring little cat for company. Contentment reigned!

The weather was very wet that year, how glad we were that Toast was safe and warm at home. Once when there were floods everywhere, we picked a different route home after school, a dip in the road held a small pond of water; it looked alright, so engaging low gear we ploughed on through. "The water's coming in Mum!" they shouted. "Lift your feet up!" said I and kept going, there was nothing else for it, when we surfaced on the other side, the floor of the little mini was awash, however we discovered little holes whose rubber bungs had been pushed out, and the water simply ran out again!!! We thought that was rather neat! and drove home none the worse! However she didn't like damp weather and often refused to start in the morning, until the man from the garage fitted a kind of apron under the bonnet, to keep the worst of the weather out. Until that time there was the embarrassment of having to find some-one to give me a push!! When the children were older and consequently bigger and stronger, it was a great relief as all four of them together could get things started in fine style! When David grew big enough to change a tyre, and offered to do so, he was so professional about it, I felt my worries were over. However, that was later, and meanwhile the mini had an eventful life. Once the windscreen wipers gave up in the middle of our local town, it had been raining cats and dogs all day, and we had to get home, luckily one of the boys had a long piece of string in his pocket, which we tied to the right-hand wiper, and we drove home very carefully with the window open, and me pulling on the string to clear the windscreen at judicious intervals, trying to smile cheerfully at those who stared in disbelief at what they saw! Once we got stuck in first gear in the same town and had to edge very slowly home like that. Our local garage was wonderful they seemed to be able to mend it every time! Though not for ever perhaps. One entry on the calendar reads "To garage for oil change - left car as wheels may drop off! Collected at one. Falls to bits at six!" but we had it back next day, and on we went!

It was in summer on the way home from "our" beach that we were horrified by a sudden terrible noise, heralding Trouble, when the mini came to a halt we all jumped out to see what it was - the exhaust was hanging down and dragging on the ground. How lucky, that in a mini like ours, one can so often find a bit of string! We managed to tie it up, and went carefully home through the lanes; it made an awful noise had the silencer gone too?

Gradually we sold off all the surplus furniture we had in the garage, everything in fact that we didn't actually use, and this helped towards the garage bills, and although I always felt that they never charged a penny more than they had to, it was always a major catastrophe when the car broke down.

On the way to collect the children one day, I popped into the second-hand wood place (stocks of old wooden doors etc, and useful things like nuts and bolts, locks and door handles}, and outside they had put a big new store area filled with pieces of wood they were throwing out, I went to enquire and was told they were left there for anyone who wanted some. I asked if I might have a load to take home and was told cheerfully to come and help myself, anytime! Good Heavens, how wonderful! I filled the back of the mini right away for our fire that evening, and from then on for as long as it was available collected a mini-full at regular intervals after dropping the children off at school.

It was lovely sitting by our fire, cosy on a winter's evening, for the children watching Children's Hour on T.V., and for me after I had bathed the two youngest; read the bed-time story; kissed them all goodnight, and then done the last milking; carried the brimming buckets of clean water from the kitchen down to the goat-house; distributed armfuls of hay from where it was stored off the ground, in the garage, and any buckets of oats which were still needed. Then I could get my own supper, and sit and watch the news with Toast by my side, with the crackling of the logs providing a kind of company too. However, it was a bit upsetting seeing the wood which had taken so long to collect and saw up, going up in flames so fast!! The wood which came from the second-hand wood store went up even faster, but certainly ensured that the fire always got going well, and then had to be judiciously mixed with our logs, and now and again, when it rained a lot and wood was sodden, or I hadn't been able to find any, I drove the little mini to the local coal-merchants, and he would sell us a sack or two of coal and load it in for me, but we hadn't really anywhere to keep it and it was an extra expense.

At this time there was a lot to be heard about wood-stoves, they sounded amazing, economical to run, and very good at warming the entire house apparently, the whole stove got hot and gave off a good heat, whilst burning the wood very slowly. They sounded so good that we visited a "Stove Shop" in a little country town not far from us. It had every type of stove, some were for cooking on and others just for heating, most were matt black and looked old fashioned in a comfortable sort of way, some were coloured in warm red, or green stove enamel and were jewel-like in their beauty, others had dear little doors in front with windows in them so you could see the flames. It was most exciting, until I began to wonder about the price and looked at the labels hanging from them! Working my way down the scale didn't get me very far, even the cheapest was quite beyond me, they were out of the question so that was that!

Then one day, after filling the car with the wonderful off-cuts of wood, the owner of the yard asked me if I was burning it on my wood-stove, and upon hearing that we didn't have such a thing, told me he was selling one he had "in the back" as they were installing gas heating now. He took me in and showed me a dear little black stove, the price he wanted for it was much more reasonable than buying new, and I was tempted, but worried about how to fit it in as it would stick out beyond our hearth. In the end they threw in a nice big paving stone to stand it on, and came out and fitted it into place for me. It was very good and warmed the room, on far less wood than an open fire and I didn't have to buy any more coal! The only drawback was that one could no longer watch the flames, and one found oneself concentrating on the tiny hole in the front door which glowed a comforting red! Nevertheless, the little stove served us well, and because it got hot all over, one often came down in the morning to a nice warm room, with the odd spark amongst the ash which on weekends could be rekindled for the daytime too.

Chapter 16
Clogs

As the evenings grew darker Daisy and Parsley both began to get restless, luckily no-one seemed to be aware of the plaintive calls coming from the goat-house, perhaps it was far enough away from all the little houses. Certainly we heard nothing until I went down to the end of the garden. Although it is the springtime when most of the animal and bird kingdom's thoughts turn towards romance, goats, it seems, have to be different. Parsley was too young anyway, and we intended to do all the right things for her, to ensure that she was as healthy and well built as a well brought up goat can be. This meant not taking her to a male goat, until her second year, so it was lucky for us that she seemed rather half-hearted about the whole thing, and only called occasionally, for a shortish time. Not so, Daisy, who, for several days each month became more and more insistent, the counsel of perfection was that she too was supposed to wait a year, but she had other ideas. Whenever I took her out to be milked I had to keep a very firm hold on her collar, she was quite determined to grab the first chance she could, to dash off and find the nearest male goat for herself, as we seemed to be so obtuse! In the end the whole thing became such a problem that I gave in, and took her to the nearest good male I could find, just before the fireworks at the school on November 5th! You have to go when the goat dictates, which as a rule is never particularly convenient for the owner! After that, horribly aware of the smell of male goat everywhere, I decided we'd give the school bonfire a miss, this year! I then cleaned the car as well as possible, and we all went off to a village not far from where we used to live, I'd quite by chance seen in the local paper that they were holding a village bonfire night in a big field, it was out in the country, open to the public, and you bought tickets at the gate. The people selling the tickets were nice and friendly and if we walked about in a miasma of goat scent, no-one appeared to notice. In fact there was a strong smell of cow about so it probably all mingled nicely. We were able to buy delicious hot-dogs, and the fireworks were lovely, it turned out to be a magical evening, and afterwards we walked back up the lane in the velvety dark enjoying the feeling of being back in the real country-side again, and as we reached our little car we heard an owl hooting in nearby trees, a perfect end to the day.

Now we could look forward to a fairly peaceful time I thought, the two goats would be contented with each other's company till the Spring, Mary was staying with the flock on Mr. Toms farm until then so I could concentrate on the family, getting ready for Christmas etc. Production had slowed down now, - we were getting much less milk, Daisy would have to dry off and conserve her strength for the new kid, but there was frozen milk in the freezer. Egg-laying was becoming non-existent, but goats and hens must all be well looked after so production gets off to a flying start in the spring we hope.

Indoors, Toast had blossomed, having found her voice, she proved to have more of a vocabulary than we ever expected, and had become the heart of the house, always there to welcome us home. She runs down the stairs to greet us with a bright little bird-like chirrup, which she also does if meeting one unexpectedly in or out of the house. Occasionally she will give a tiny scarcely audible mew as a request, and at times a very insistent MEW, accompanied by a very definite GLARE, and even lashing her lovely luxuriant tail, when one has been working for far too long, and ought to sit down and provide a lap, for Goodness Sake! All is sweetness and light once one has complied, and she jumps lightly up to settle herself cosily upon you! She seems to have great understanding, and if anyone is in need of a little comfort, theirs is the bed you will find her on. Her purring is amazing it can be low and fairly quiet, and continuous, re-affirming her pleasure in the company if one of us sits quietly beside her, doing home-work or reading, but when she is very happy and contented and wants you to be too, the gentle rumbling will grow and grow till it seems to fill the house with contentment.

One night when David and Ben were in their beds on each side of their room, I went in to say Good-night, Toast was lying apparently asleep on David's bed. Ben not realising it was so late let out a wail, "Toast hasn't come to me yet, I want her on my bed! It's my turn." David was inclined to argue as Toast was asleep. "It's not fair!" Ben began, but Toast suddenly sat bolt up-right, regarded Ben closely for a moment, then with a flying bound she was across the room, landing at the foot of his bed, she marched up the length of it, stared into his eyes and immediately settled down beside him, kneading him gently with her huge paws as her purrs welled up within her, until the whole room was filled with the lovely sound, and peace descended.

Checking back to the calendars of those years, upon which so much was recorded of each season's happenings - in the garden, with the animals, even every dental and doctor's visit, trips we made and visitors, it is odd to find that the Christmas period is generally blank. I think this is indicative of the sort of winter hibernation my friend Maria complained of, when she said she would rather live in one room in London, than in a house in the country, when everything got so dark and lonely. In fact once her children left the school, they, and many others like her left the area and went back to the towns from whence they had come. To each his own, for me living in a town is like being a battery hen, I feel as if I cannot breathe, and am thoroughly miserable!

Christmas has always been a truly wonderful time of year, the preparations for which alone, engender a magical aura throughout the house. The children still made visits to friends though, and often two of them would be away for the night with different families, whilst the two youngest spent the day away, so one was busy dropping them all off at various locations, or collecting them again! Equally often they would be collected, giving me more time to make the Christmas pudding, the Cake, stuffing for the turkey and so on, these things had to be done in December, a less hectic month. Then again their friends would come to us for the day, I remember a horde of them trooping into the kitchen one year to stir the pudding and make a wish, after it had been standing all night to mull, before being put into its bowls to be cooked in the pressure cooker. I also made lashings of gravy from the vegetable water, frozen each day for this purpose, (one could always add some of the water from the giblets on Christmas Eve), Bread Sauce, from a white loaf bought specially, as brown doesn't look very appetising! Though we never eat anything but wholemeal, and I never cook with anything but wholemeal flour, even the white sauce seems fine, and so much better for everyone! For the pudding we have our version of hard sauce, which is delicious, butter and sugar beaten up with a little sherry, if I didn't do advance preparations, they'd never get done - how wonderful it is to have a freezer to pop everything into all ready. We could always count on Granny to give us some sherry in good time for Christmas, as she made her sauce the same way, she was also responsible for the turkey, which was terribly kind. She would always join us for lunch on Christmas

Day, and bring one of her neighbours who lived alone which helped us to make it a real celebration, after Church on Christmas morning.

We still went out every day, for walks, often through the woods, dragging back logs and collecting chestnuts, finding Ivy to drape round the house or twigs in pleasing shapes, Chestnut and Beech husks were good, and I could set my team to painting them in gold and silver, on rainy afternoons, and we would all make decorations out of coloured crepe paper, and transform the entire house which is a very good pastime in bad weather. They grew out of all that quite soon, but still helped with branches of fir or holly, and decorating the tree which gave me time for other things. We found that if we dashed out to buy a tree on Christmas Eve the price had just about reached our level, and we could get a small one and stand it on a stool to make it seem larger! Though a memory persists of using a fir branch one year, and once a big bare one we had found lying in the woods, we hung the baubles on it, but it was not the same!

One night before Christmas there was something on T.V which we could all enjoy, so for once as a special treat I told everyone they could all stay up to see it. It had been a cold wintery day, dark and louring with a leaden sky, and I felt we could do with a little cheering up. By tea-time it was beginning to look like snow, and after supper while everyone got ready for bed, I fed and watered the goats as the first flakes began to float earthwards, they were big and fluffy and came down faster and faster, the sort that mean business, the garden and the little fir-tree outside the dining-room were covered in no time. The four children came thundering down the stairs in their dressing-gowns, their eyes shining, their faces lit up with the delight of it "Mum, Mum, have you seen the snow?" "You should see it out of my window, its going into great drifts, already!" "It's all building up on my window-sill!" "We'll be able to toboggan tomorrow!" "Good Gracious!" I said, "Maybe we'll have a white Christmas!" They were ecstatic at this festive turn of events. Though I closed the curtains to keep out the cold, stoked up the fire and we all settled down cosily on our long sofa to enjoy the evening's entertainment, with Toast lying on first one lap, and then another. By nine thirty the programme came to an end, the two youngest were sleepy by now and we trooped upstairs. I'd settled Kate cosily into her bed and walked into the boy's room, John was in his own small room peering out at the snow, but in here there was something odd, it looked like a huge damp patch on the ceiling, was it a shadow? How unobservant, not to have noticed it before! It was worrying me, I called John and we all looked at it, no-one could remember it being there before. Oh No! Was that a drip? John and David announced with one breath, that they'd go up into the roof and have a look. "Oh dear! I suppose you'd better, but you must put your trousers on over your pyjamas, a sweater and socks." What would I have done without them, luckily they rose to the occasion magnificently, treating it cheerfully like a big adventure.

Once they had dressed, over their pyjamas, they swung themselves up into the roof, "Wow - look at that!" exclaimed John, " A mountain!" shouted David, "Come and look, Ben!" "Shh! You'll disturb, Kate!" I interjected hastily, Ben needed a kitchen chair to stand on, so did I as I tried to see into the attic. There was the tip of a big pile of snow; it must have blown in under the tiles. "We'll have to form a chain, I'll get some bowls and that big plastic bucket, and a shovel, and you two shovel it into them, and I'll hurl it out of the back door." Luckily we had more than one shovel, one for the chicken house, and one for the fireplace. As fast as John and David filled the containers, Ben passed them to me and I ran up and down the stairs, hurling it out of the back door. It formed a big pile out there - a surprising amount! We worked so fast we did not get cold, and when they pronounced the attic clear we spread plastic rubbish sacks around in case it happened again, and left the bowls up there too. Thank goodness, it had stopped snowing by now. In fact strangely, that never happened again, and it was thought amongst my neighbours later that the wind had been coming from an unusual direction that night!

Next morning Kate was delighted to find the snow all piled up, the beginnings of a really good snowman! They used tiny pieces of coal for his eyes, a carrot for his nose, and even a moth eaten old scarf for his muffler. Then John and David dashed off while the younger ones were otherwise engaged to see if the slope above the house had enough snow on it to toboggan, and reported that it looked good, some people had used it already! Unfortunately we only had three tin trays, so we found a plastic rubbish sack and they agreed to take it in turns with that as well. The snow had hardened up considerably, and apparently it worked quite well. "There was somebody else up there using a sack as well!"

Ben reported, when they all came home, soaking wet and happy and ravening for food!

Once the lanes were passable, Granny arrived bringing an old cap for the snowman! She would either visit us most week-ends, or we went to her if I felt the children had been having a rather boring time; that was my worry, how to make sure each of them got enough attention when I was so busy, maybe it helped to have someone else to listen to them once a week as well, - they loved to visit her, and David often popped across the lane to see her neighbour as she said it cheered her up.

The snow had gone and the children were at school, when Mr. Toms rang to ask if we wanted Mary back. Good Heavens! This time I went off to collect her on my own. Mr. Toms and I walked up the field to where the flock were grazing. Oh dear! Would she remember me? Feeling bad because I really couldn't tell one sheep from another, when we got nearer I called her name, several sheep lifted their heads and calmly regarded us without moving, I called again, one seemed to look at me intently, so I continued to call. "Here she comes!" said Mr. Toms, and suddenly I saw her moving out from the flock, then she began to trot towards us, reaching me she nuzzled my hand, then wheeling round she led the way to the field gate and the mini parked outside it, Mr. Toms opened the gate and Mary and I hurried through, she waited by the door till I got it open, then promptly jumped in and lay down contentedly in the clean straw, and that was the second time in our lives the farmer told me he would never have believed it, had he not seen it with his own eyes!

I thought privately that she was determined not to be left behind a second time! After that we always had her back after her visit to the ram, it seemed that was what she preferred though truly she was treated with special consideration, whenever she went to the farm. Three times a year she visited, to be dipped, to be shorn, and again for her nuptials. She never showed any sign of not wanting to go, and seemed happy to see the flock again. Mr. Toms had a blind sheep which he always looked out for, who would find her way by positioning herself in the centre of the flock, and moving with it. So when Mary was there he kept an eye on the two of them. She certainly always came down to the mini with alacrity when we fetched her, and produced her babies with no fuss which was a blessing. This year, in due time she produced just one lamb, and we named him Apple!

Eventually when winter was gone, and all over the garden the spring flowers appeared, and we revelled in the return of warm sunshine, Daisy chose this opportune moment to produce more twins. I had not picked her mate with special care this time, now that we had the impeccable Parsley to breed from; this had been a case of any port in a storm, so we got a big surprise when we went down to the goat-house that morning, to find Daisy with one white and one black kid beside her in the straw. Investigation proved that the white one was a Fred, and the little black one was a girl - she was very sweet, she had touches of white on her ears, and face and little white socks, while under her chin were two little black toggles - she was to all appearances, a British Alpine! Then we noticed that Fred, although white had two little white toggles! As Daisy and Parsley were British Saanens it was rather fun having a varied herd for a while, I didn't plan on keeping either of them permanently. The little black kid was extremely gentle and very shy, David took to her from the very beginning, and she to him. We decided to give her a flower name like her mother, and somebody suggested Columbine which seemed to suit her rather well. When we eventually let them out in the paddock, with

Parsley, and Mary and Apple it was delightful to see them all enjoying the sun. The calendar notes - "all the animals skipping about happily"!

The routine went on as before, Daisy, Parsley, and Mary went up the footpath to browse a different area each day, whilst their progeny skipped about on our fenced-in lawn, which was definitely a paddock now that the grass had grown quite rough and long. Columbine dainty and very pretty with her black coat which was getting a definite healthy sheen these days, had no horns, these having been removed by the vet; using a local anaesthetic, when she was a few days old, Fred, who whilst he had two little horns was still nevertheless quite gentle, and very picturesque, because as he grew little black hairs appeared between the white on the top of his head and down his neck, and Apple the little fat lamb did not look like his mother either, as his head and face were a dark chocolaty brown. When the three white adults joined them later, it made for a delightful picture I thought, especially as we tied the brilliantly coloured garden parasol to one of the posts to provide a shady corner. We situated a bucket of clean water at one end, carefully wedged with large stones, so that it couldn't be knocked over, and each day I brought armfuls of grass, branches, or swathes of ivy, or brambles which I tied to the side for them to browse on.

One day David was in the paddock carrying an armful of succulent greenery to a quieter corner for the timid little Columbine, having deposited it, he knelt down to tie his shoelace. The little black kid looked over her shoulder at him, and clearly feeling playful suddenly took it into her head to prance over and take a flying leap onto his back! He said it felt exactly like little clogs, clopping onto him, and promptly christened her Clogs! She loved David, and always expected him to play; leaping onto his back became her party trick until she became too heavy and her clogs rather painful! She would also lie quietly in his lap when she'd had enough exercise, and let him gently stroke her and fondle her ears. She grew up into the gentlest of the goats and of course stayed with us, and had a happy life as one of the family from then on.

It became apparent that my idea of acquiring a place that was suitable for us to have a herd of goats, and sell the milk, and make yogurt, and cheese commercially just wasn't going to happen, but I had already attended a course on cheese-making, on a commercial goat farm, which was both informative and fun. The herd there could roam over a wide area of field and woods, and came back to their stalls when called, it seemed such a happy arrangement that many years later when the children grew up, and I gave up goat-keeping I transferred Parsley to them, feeling she would appreciate the freedom, I don't think she would have missed us at all. She was a fine goat but unlike the others didn't seem to have a lot between the ears!

Until then we just kept to the three adult goats, breeding from two on one year, and from one the next. Mary produced lambs, and we had the hens, and our own fruit and vegetables. However, this is no way to make money, it is labour intensive, and you might have to be mad to do it, but I was with my children as I wanted to be, and we were healthy and happy. I felt as if we had dropped off the world, apart from all the kind people around us each of whom performed unexpected acts of kindness, sometimes anonymously. So often we came home to find sacks of vegetables for the goats on the doorstep. Goat-keepers occasionally left oats, sometimes there was wood for the fire, and Richard and Hilary whom we first called upon when we wondered about getting our first goat, came with goat treats, vegetables, and apples in season, and Hilary was always there for a chat on the telephone that sent me on my way refreshed.

Chapter 17

Another One?

After the arrival of the baby animals, life continued apace, it was always extremely busy, never a dull moment, "What wouldn't I give for a bit of good old boredom!" Was a craven thought that occasionally raised its ugly head, hastily squashed! Every year there came a time when they all had to be bottle fed, three times a day, if their mothers had fed them for a while first. Daisy always gets rid of her offspring as soon as possible! Apple on his own was alright, but when Mary started producing triplets, they had to be fed too! Once they had all gone life was slightly less hectic. Till harvesting and preserving begins, but it's a change of routine, which is as good as a rest!

Summer was still with us, reluctant to depart, though it would not be too long before the first signs of Autumn came upon us, Daisy, Parsley, Clogs and Mary our permanent four, were all up the footpath, where they browsed according to what was in season, now they were knee high in leafy plants, the goats pulled at the hog-weed leaves and chewed contentedly. Our vegetables had done well, and the children were at school. I was enjoying sitting in the garden on the small lawn under the shade of the cherry tree near the house, stringing runner-beans, some for supper, and many more to be blanched, thrown into iced water, and when cool frozen for the winter. It was very peaceful, a gentle breeze moved the leaves of the trees, and then departed, I sliced away industriously, and gradually became aware that I was not alone, I looked up and there sitting bolt upright under the small fir, was a large stripey tabby cat with piercing green eyes!

Now some time ago I had been making my way towards our gate with Daisy, Parsley, and Clogs on their chains which was a bit much to control, but it was late and we did not have to go on the road, so I risked it, when a car to my horror pulled hurriedly into our lay-by, right up to us, causing the goats to pull like mad and tie themselves in knots. The woman in it jumped out, oblivious of the mayhem she was causing, and as my arms threatened to leave their sockets agitatedly asked me if I had seen a large cat. Hoping against hope that she had not turned up to claim Toast after all this time, I asked her what sort of cat? She replied that it was a sort of stripey cat, and well, she loved him. At that I said that of course if I saw him I'd let her know, so she gave me her address, and departed. How long ago that was I couldn't think, was it days or weeks? I must fetch her at once, moving gently but quickly not to frighten the cat away, I dashed through the kitchen grabbing the address off the notice board where I'd pinned it, and calling to my neighbour asked her to keep an eye out for Mary who might come home when she got bored, and had to be let into the paddock. I drove straight to the house, but it seemed odd, the front door was wide open and though I called and knocked there was obviously no-one there, indeed now I noticed there was an air of dereliction about the place. Crossing the road I found a woman sitting out in the sun, I told her the story of the cat, but she gave me to understand that the woman's cat had been found, and the family had moved away. Just as well, because when I got home, the stripey one had gone.

When he re-appeared a few days later he was lying under the little fir, blinking lazily at me as I brought Daisy up to be milked. When the boys went up the footpath at the week-end they reported meeting a huge tabby cat in the woods. So the appearances went on for a time,

I didn't touch him, or talk to him for a while, as I was afraid he'd guess I loved animals, and I didn't want to encourage him, thinking he probably only needed time to settle into his new home where-ever that may be, as no-one in our neck of the woods seemed to know anything about him. Next time I sat outside to string beans, he stood under the tree and we looked at each other, then he gave a little totter, and seemed to almost fall down. I felt terrible, he needed our help, he'd never asked - just came and patiently waited. I ran indoors, and returned with a small serving of cat-food and a saucer of goats-milk - he cleaned the plates, lay down and went to sleep.

From then on he came each day, and made it clear that he wanted to come indoors, but I shut the door as I couldn't face a cat fight, patiently he continued to wait - and when Toast saw him she became, on the instant a hell-cat! Her ears went flat, her whole appearance changed, flattened and hardened, as he walked purposefully up to the glass, and stared dispassionately in. Toast was incandescent with rage, ears flat, spitting and cursing volubly, the tabby regarded her for a long moment and then calmly walked away, and lay down under the fir tree, blinking lazily. He was never anything but courteous and calm, I continued to feed him, but told both cats they would have to sort out what to do themselves! Maybe they understood, as from then on the door remained open as usual, most of the day, there were no cat fights, and the stripey cat didn't rush things, sometimes Toast sat on the mat inside the kitchen, and the stranger sat on the path near the steps, both staring into space! Then the day came, when Toast was to be seen sitting like a tea-cosy on the grass, and the other was in the kitchen! Though he left later, she appeared not to notice his departure! They seemed to have come to an arrangement eventually, as daily, Toast left the house to sleep in some cosy spot in the garden, while allowing the tabby into the kitchen, though I never witnessed the actual change-over! By the time I went to fetch the children from school, she was back indoors, and he had gone, though sometimes at night the shadow under the fir seemed darker than usual and I was sure that he was there, feeling safe in our garden perhaps.

One morning after the goat chores, when I went up to make the beds, a huge stripey form was stretched out fully, on Kate's bed; he was over three feet long! (I know because one day I measured him). He looked at me with his lazy expression and I sat beside him to make him welcome and get to know him. He purred gently as his head was stroked, and as my hand moved down his great long back, he suddenly whipped over and grabbed it in both his front paws with all his claws out! Stalemate, they were very sharp and it seemed unwise to move, thinking he was testing me I sat quite still and talked gently to him. He regarded me out of watchful eyes, emerald green and quite piercing, his fur was wonderfully silvery between the big black stripes, and his tail lashed gently on the bed, he was ready for anything! We stayed like that for a while until he was sure that I wouldn't panic, or be rough, and then he released me, I continued to sit still, and he relaxed, letting me see the wonderful butterfly shape between his shoulder blades. What a beautiful creature he was - the cat that walked by himself - asleep on Kate's bed.

That evening he stayed - he just went to sleep and made no attempt to move, I closed the sitting-room door on Toast while I fetched the children, not liking to leave them alone together so soon, in case of trouble, though in fact there never was any. Kate and the boys too were thrilled to hear that the tabby had apparently moved in and was actually asleep on Kate's bed, "What shall we call him?" Ben suddenly asked, and we spent the rest of the journey trying to think up something apposite, that we could call out easily when we wanted him to come in for supper, for instance. Eventually we agreed on Stripey, although I didn't feel that was quite good enough, and finally we added O'Riley for good measure. This is Stripey O'Riley, we would say when introducing him to our friends, it seemed more fitting. They all trooped upstairs to welcome the new member of the family, and he opened his green eyes blinked lazily at them, and went back to sleep again. I warned them not to touch him when he was asleep, because of his sharp claws, but they were not likely to disturb a sleeping animal, it was one of those things that was just not done, as far as we were concerned. They are not stuffed toys, and should be treated with loving respect!

However, for the first few weeks it was very clear that he had been living rough, although he slept on the couch, he was on the qui vive all the time, one ear listening, and awake and watchful in an instant if a car went by outside, or at any new noise. The first time that he deigned to come and sleep on the sofa, we were all there, by the fire or over by the table and he had it to himself for a moment, and looked as if he didn't know quite how to proceed, he had jumped up and we all watched him, suddenly he lay down, without folding up in the usual way, but by simply falling sideways, legs all stiff - and missed the couch completely, we sprang, and literally caught him, like a big plate on our outstretched arms!! He purred as we all settled down together, but after that we kept an eye on him ready to catch him, whenever he approached the couch, but luckily it never happened again, and he settled down contentedly like a normal cat after that.

"Are you sure he hasn't escaped from the zoo?" the neighbours used to ask, "I've never seen one that size, he can't be an ordinary cat!" No indeed, although cats that are left with their mothers and not separated too early, and are decently fed, and not pulled about too much as kittens, grow into better animals than many one sees today, we never felt that Stripey O'Riley was in any way ordinary!

Stripey O'Riley took us all over I believe, Kate was just about seven when he arrived and he was still with us as confidante and companion when she went off to university, and the boys were grown up and had jobs. He must have been a young cat when he arrived, and grew up with them; Toast was always gentle and quiet. But Stripey could be one of the boys, as they grew up they had this thing about play-fighting, they would chase each other through the house, swing round the newel post at the bottom of the stairs and thunder up them, Stripey soon joined in, he would hear them coming and lie in wait, then make a dash towards them attempting to catch their ankles as they leapt for the stair. "Quick there's Stripey! Quick!" If he didn't catch one of them he would dash up the stairs after them, and be in the middle of the melee at the top, my heart would be in my mouth, but they all loved him dearly and were aware of his presence, soon he would be lying back "like an Eastern Potentate" as my mother put it, purring and grooming himself on David's bed, no doubt satisfied that he had sorted them all out. Although he enjoyed "playing rough" with the boys, he always treated Kate and me much more gently.

He would often accompany any of us who walked up the footpath, following stealthily and then breaking into a trot to overtake us, and suddenly dash for the nearest tree, climb out of reach and peer down, "What if he can't get down?" I asked anxiously, the first time. "He'll be alright!" said John, "He often does it!" Then a thundering of hooves (!) as this time he made his presence felt, and rushed ahead with his tail, in a rakish sideways

"C" and dashed up another tree ahead. Once when we came out upon the green at the end, he led the way along the little footpath towards the stile at the other end, it must have been early summer, and to our surprise he suddenly launched himself high into the air and landed in the long grass at the side, in a cacophony of terror a female pheasant rose from beneath his paws, losing only a handful of feathers, and leaving him growling furiously to himself.

Once following me into the garage one day, he rose in a leap that would have reached my shoulder, and batted a poor little wren that had tried to fly past us to the door, to my sorrow it was dead when I picked it up. I had instinctively cried "Oh No Stripey!" when I saw what he was jumping at, and now I picked him up gently, "No Stripey, poor wren." I held him in my arms, and let him divine my sorrow. He relaxed against me and I carried him out of the garage. Then I buried the wren. It's not right to blame a cat for doing what is in its nature, I knew, and didn't, but he understood and never attempted to catch another bird. Though every spring he went up into the fields and brought back a baby rabbit each day until they got too big, this he laid out by the kitchen door, quite dead. I praised him, and told him what a good and clever cat he was, he had to do this perhaps, and he ate all but the tail and part of the intestine! Though he still expected and got supper at the usual time!

Worried that the cats were not getting enough to eat, we weighed him one day, by standing on the scale and holding him. He weighed nearly a stone, though Toast was a little lighter, being smaller.

Of course he could move as silently and unobtrusively as a shadow, as I knew well, when last thing at night I picked my way down the garden path with only the stars above for light, when he had not come home, not wanting to go to bed till he was safe inside, and standing there willing him to return, - and no sign - not calling, it was so late neighbours were all asleep - no lights anywhere, thank Goodness even the street lights went out at this time, my eyes now used to the dark - no Stripey, and at long last turning reluctantly to go in, and something made me jump out of my skin, as it brushed the back of my legs! Then he walked companionably back up the path beside me to where the light from the kitchen door welcomed us in. Conversely once when the house was quiet, with only me upstairs, I heard loud and heavy steps coming up, had I left the door open? Who on earth could it be? Screwing up my courage and venturing into the dark passage, only Stripey was there sitting at the top. We never discovered how on earth he could make himself sound as if he was wearing hob-nailed boots! He did it quite frequently when he wished to attract attention!

When they grew up into their late teens, the boys would come in to find Stripey lying on the arm-chair, "Hi Stripey!" Someone would say genially, putting down a carelessly caressing hand, Stripey would grab it, ears back, mouth and front paws grappling, and back paws kicking simultaneously, as he hung on to it! "Ow! Stripey that hurts!" but he didn't do any damage, and having bashed whichever of my huge sons up, he would contentedly curl up on their laps. Sometimes you could come into the room to find them in a row on the sofa, with Stripey spreading his long length across the lot of them!

He saw me through thick and thin, late at night when the house was quiet and all were asleep, if I had worries and a bad day, and the house was cold and damp, and I could see no way of coping, Stripey would be there like the rock of Gibraltar, steady and true, lying there warm and gently purring, he would raise his head and look at one, how could one disintegrate and give in to despair, it just wouldn't be fair. I buried my face in his side, and he waited patiently, purring still, "Dear Stripey, what would I do without you?" I said lovingly, my composure still intact, things would seem better in the morning.

He adored Kate and in later years when John went off to university, being the first as usual to blaze a trail. Kate moved into his little room, and Stripey would still spend time on her bed. When she went up to do her homework, like most cats he thought the best thing to do would be to sit on her books, she loved him too and he knew it but being Kate, "Don't even think about it Cat!" said she and with one paw half-way there - he didn't. He just sank down where he was as close to her as possible, and stared into space.

I think really it's not fair if one is out all day to have only one cat, they need the company of another, I always hoped that one day we would come in to find Toast and Stripey curled up together cosily in the same chair, but they never did. Toast had a quite different character she was loved just as much and loved us too, sitting on our laps in turn in the evenings purring her loud comforting purrs and kneading us with her big paws, she grew even more beautiful as time went by, with longish hair, black, mahogany, and gold and her ears had little points of palest gold hair, which used to shine in the summer sun, her tail fat and luxuriant, almost prehensile as she wrapped it lovingly around ones wrist or ankle. Feminine and dainty in her manner, she did not wander far afield like Stripey whose territory encompassed not only our house and garden, but the fields and woods beside it. He occasionally worried me by also crossing the main road, and jumping down to the field on the other side, when he returned he would leap up what appeared to be a six foot wall, in one bound, and stalk majestically back across the road, occasionally bringing the traffic to a stop to allow him to do so in safety! I had to let him wander at will, much as I would have liked to keep him safe, this was a cat who walked by himself, and he had chosen to honour us with the task of providing for his comforts, but he was a law unto himself. Everyone seemed to get to know and care about him, and we were so lucky that he lived with us till he reached a ripe old age.

Toast being a home-body, meant that I never stood in the garden late at night willing her to come home, she would be curled up cosily and comfortingly indoors whenever needed, but she liked the garden, and occasionally sat on the front door-step. Her bravery was her claim to fame, when once she was found sitting outside the entrance to the footpath, near our gate, David was in the house when a worried man knocked at our door one day, "Is that your cat, over there?" He asked pointing, "Would you mind moving it? My dog won't go past it!" There he discovered poor Toast, bravely out-facing a large and vociferously barking Alsatian. She knew that it would be dangerous to run, and stayed put, fluffed up to appear larger than life and out-staring the great dog, till David went out and picked her up and brought her back to safety, growling under her breath, and glaring balefully at her tormentor.

We now had a well-rounded family, with four outside animals, and two in the house to keep us company. When winter was upon us and the weather got colder and colder, and we piled all the blankets we possessed on the children's beds, and all our windows were so covered with ice each morning that it was impossible to see out, it was so cold that it didn't melt and formed wonderful designs like ferns growing up from the bottom and covering the whole window, when the sun shone through them we wished we had a camera it was so very beautiful. However, we discovered to our amazement that it was on the inside of the windows! The two cats made it clear that under the circumstances they would sleep on my bed, till things returned to normal.

I was in the kitchen late in the evening, filling a hot water bottle, when there was a noise at the door leading into the hall, turning expecting to see a child who had woken in the night, through the glass panelled top half, I saw no-one, must have been imagination! The noise came again, and as I looked I saw the handle very definitely being depressed - it couldn't be, even little Kate's head could normally be seen through the panel, but down the handle definitely went before my horrified gaze, as frighteningly, the door swung open. It was Stripey O'Riley who stood up and pulled it down with his paw, coming in for a last snack, before moving like a shadow up the stairs, where he settled himself at the foot of my bed.

Toast slept near the top, and I drifted off to sleep like a child with its stuffed toys, though I'd never had much time for them in my youth, how wonderful was the real thing, I thought as Toast's purrs provided a lullaby, and she apparently neither moved nor ceased as I woke happily to rolling purrs in the morning, and a new day began.

www.ingramcontent.com/pod-product-compliance
Ingram Content Group UK Ltd.
Pitfield, Milton Keynes, MK11 3LW, UK
UKHW041843200726
13854UKWH00005BA/1949